THE POEMS OF PHŒBE CAREY

NEW YORK
HURST & COMPANY
Publishers

PHŒBE CAREY

CONTENTS

	PAGE
A Story	7
The Lovers	15
The Followers of Christ	19
Sonnets	24
Sympathy	27
Memories	30
Moralizings	31
Dreaming of Heaven	34
Morning Thoughts	35
The Mariner's Bride	36
The Prisoner's Last Night	38
Song of the Heart	40
Man Believes the Strong	42
The Homesick Peasant	43
Homes for All	46
Harvest Gathering	48
Prayer	50
Life is Not Vanity	52
Burial Hymn	54
Song of the Reformed	54
The Cold Water Army	56
Coming Home	57
Parting and Meeting	59
The Reefer	61
A Time to Die	62
Love at the Grave	63
Strength of Sin	65
The Place of Graves	67
Fears	68
Melody	70
The Women at the Sepulchre	71
The Watcher	72
Chalmers	74
Song	76
The Ills of Life	77
The Bride	78
Remembrance	80
Entering Heaven	82
Our Baby	84
Our Friend	84
The Outcast	87
At the Water's Edge	88
Chances	91
The Convict's Child	94
The Life of Trial	96
Death of a Friend	97
Death Scene	98
Dead	99
The Watcher's Story	101
Resolves	106
Prophecies	109
Dreams	110
The Confession	111
The Poem	113
To One Who Sang of Love	114
Archie	115
Maiden Fears	117
The Unguarded Moment	120
Burning the Letters	121

	PAGE
Nelly	123
A Lament	126
The Lullaby	128
Left Alone	130
The Retrospect	131
One Shall Be Taken	133
The Brothers	134
Remorse	137
Prophecy	138
The Consecration	139
Drawing Water	141
The Dreamer	142
Solemnity of Life	144
My Blessings	145
Sabbath Thoughts	147
Nearer Home	148
Hymn	149
Sowing Seed	150
The Baptism	151
The Christian Woman	154
The Hosts of Thought	156
Our Homestead	160
The Book of Poems	162
To Frank	163
Morning	164
Dawn	165
PARODIES.	
Martha Hopkins	166
Worser Moments	170
The Annoyer	172
Samuel Brown	174
Granny's House	175
The Day is Done	181
John Thompson's Daughter	182
Girls Were Made to Mourn	184
To Inez	187
To Mary	189
The Change	190
He Never Wrote Again	192
The Soiree	193
The City Life	195
The Marriage of Sir John Smith	197
Ballad of the Canal	198
I Remember, I Remember	199
Jacob	200
The Wife	201
A Psalm of Life	201
"There's a Bower of Bean-Vines"	203
When Lovely Woman	204
Shakesperian Readings	204

POEMS BY PHŒBE CAREY.

A STORY.

WHILE silently our vessel glides,
  To-night, along the Adrian seas,
And while the lightly-heaving tides
  Are scarcely rippled by the
    breeze—
Thou, who, with cheek of beauty pale,
  Seem'st o'er some hidden grief to pine,
If thou wilt listen to a tale
  Of sorrow, it may lighten thine.
'Twas told me, sadly choked with tears
  My eyes, it may be, too, were wet;
For, through the shadowy lapse of years,
  My memory keeps the record yet.
And he who told it long ago,
  Though scarcely passed his manhood's
    prime

He seemed as one whose heart with wo
  Was seared and blighted ere its time.
And as he told his story o'er,
  Long vanished years came back to me;
For he had crossed my path before,
  Upon the land and on the sea.

When first by chance I saw his form,
  'Twas on the raging waves at night,
And if at all he saw the storm,
  He recked not of its angry might.
For while the dark and troubled skies
  Rung with accents of despair,
He never raised his tearful eyes,
  Nor lifted up his voice in prayer.
Once, thirsting for the cooling well,
  Beneath a fierce and burning sun,
And listening to the camel's bell,
  That music of the desert lone,
We reached a spot whose fountain made
  An Eden in that barren land;
And there, beneath the palm-tree's shade,
  We saw the lonely stranger stand.
And once, when twilight closed the flowers,
  I marked him on dark Jura's steep,
And twice amid thy sacred bowers,
  Gethsemane, I saw him weep.

But when I saw the mourner last,
  And heard the story of his woes,
'Twas where the solemn cypress cast
  Its shadow o'er man's last repose.
The sun had faded from the sky,

With all his bright and glowing bars,
And solemn clouds were gliding by,
In spectral silence o'er the stars.
And there, beside a grassy mound,
In agony for words too deep,
And eyes bent sadly on the ground,
I saw him clasp his hands and weep.
Though I had seen him on the sea
Unmoved, when all beside were pale,
And weeping in Gethsemane,
I never asked nor knew his tale.
But now, beside the tomb, at last,
By kindly looks and words, I sought
To learn the story of the past,
And win him from his troubled thought.
With lips all breathlessly apart,
He listened to each soothing word;
The chord was touched within his heart,—
The long untroubled fount was stirred.

"Companioned only by the dead,
So many years I've lived alone,
I hardly thought," he sadly said,
"To hear again a pitying tone.
But, stranger, friend, thy words are kind,
And since thou fain wouldst learn my grief,
It may be that my heart will find,
In utterance of its woes, relief.
Life's brightest scenes will I recall,
And those where shade and sunshine blend,
And, if my lips can speak it all,
I'll tell it even to the end.
My childhood! it were more than vain

To tell thee that was glad as fleet;
While innocence and youth remain,
Thou knowest that life's cup is sweet.

But when the soul of manhood beamed,
In after years, upon my brow,—

My childhood! it were more than vain
To tell thee that was glad as fleet.

(I know how darkly it is seamed
With scars of guilt and sorrow now),—
When, with the summer stars above,
And dew-drops shining in the vale,
I told the story of my love

To one who did not scorn the tale;
And when, in happiness and pride,
Such as I never knew before,
I bore her to my home a bride,
The measure of my bliss ran o'er.
Oh, in that bower of Eden blest,
I fain would linger with my song;
It irks me so to tell the rest—
The serpent did not spare it long.

"It was the eve of such a day
As on creation dawned of old,
And all along the heavenly way
The stars had set their lamps of gold.
That night I stood amid the throng
Where banquet flowers were sweetly strown,
Where wine was poured with mirth and song,
And where the smile of beauty shone
When lost in pleasure's maze, and when
My heart to reason's voice was steeled,
I tasted of the WINE-CUP, then—
I tasted, and my doom was sealed!
That night the moments passed more fleet
Than with my bride upon the hills;
That night I drank a draught more sweet
Than water from the living rills.
It is a harder task to win
The feet at first, from right astray;
Yet if but once we yield to sin,
How easy is the downward way!
Oh, if the spirit can be won
In evil ways to enter in,

That first false step may lead us on
  Through all the labyrinths of sin:
And I resisted not the power
  That drew me first towards the bowl,
While firmer every day and hour
  The chains were fastened in my soul.
I saw hope's sunny fountain fail
  In her young heart who loved me so,
As day by day, her cheek grew pale
  With vigils and with tears of wo.

'Oh, if a kind and pitying word,
  If tones so sweet as thine have been,
My erring spirit could have heard,
  They might have saved me, even then.
But no; they named with scorn my name,
  And viewed me with reproachful eyes;
For all who saw my guilt and shame
  But looked upon me to despise.
And so I left my home and hearth,
  For haunts of wickedness and sin,
And sought, in wine and stronger mirth,
  To hush the voice of God within.
I have no record in my heart
  Of how my days and weeks went by,
Save shadowy images that start
  Like spectres still before mine eye.
As something indistinct and dim
  Of sable hearse and funeral pall,
Of trailing robes and mournful hymn,
  My memory keeps—and that is all!
But when, as from a horrid dream,
  I woke, disturbed by nameless fears,

I sought beside the mountain stream
  My home so dear in earlier years.
'Twas desolate—I called my bride,
  And listened, but no answer came;
I made the hills and valleys wide
  Re-echo vainly with her name!
And when I heard a step draw near,
  And met a stranger's wondering gaze,
I asked in tones of doubt and fear,
  For that sweet friend of earlier days.
And then I followed where he led;
  And as he left that singing stream,
I glided near him with a tread
  Like guilty spirits in a dream:
He brought me to this quiet ground,
  The last repose of wo and care,
And, pointing to that grassy mound,
  He told me that MY BRIDE WAS THERE!

"I've been, for hopeless years since then,
  A wanderer on the land and sea,
And little loved the homes of men,
  Or in their busy haunts to be;
And should not now have turned to tread
  This darkest scene of all my woes,
But something in my heart has said
  My life is hastening to its close.
And now I have no wish below,
  And no request for man to keep,
If thou, who know'st my tale of wo,
  Wilt lay me by my bride to sleep."

He paused, and, blinded by his tears,
  Bowed down with sorrow dark and deep,
The hoarded agony of years

Bowed down with sorrow dark and deep.

  Broke forth, and then he ceased to weep:
But when he raised his eyes again,
  I saw, what was unseen till now,

That death, in characters too plain,
  Was written on that pallid brow.

Three little days; and then we laid
  That wreck of manhood and of pride
Beneath the gloomy cypress shade,
  To slumber with his stricken bride.

THE LOVERS.

THOU marvellest why so oft her eyes
  Fill with the heavy dew of tears—
Have I not told thee that there lies
  A shadow darkly on her years?
Life was to her one sunny whole,
  Made up of visions fancy wove,
Till that the waters of her soul
  Were troubled by the touch of love.
I knew when first the sudden pause
  Upon her spirit's sunshine fell:
Alas! I little guessed the cause,
  'Twas hidden in her heart so well.
Our lives since early infancy
  Had flowed as rills together flow,
And now to hide her thought from me
  Was bitterer than to tell its wo.

One night, when clouds with anguish black
  A tempest in her bosom woke,
She crushed the bitter tear-drops back,
  And told me that her heart was broke'

I learned it when the autumn hours
  With wailing winds around us sighed—
'Twas summer when her love's young flowers
  Burst into glorious life and died:
No—now I can remember well,
  'Twas the soft month of sun and shower;
A thousand times I've heard her tell
  The season, and the very hour:
For now, when'er the tear-drops start
  As if to ease its throbbing pain,
She leans her head upon my heart
  And tells the very tale again.

Tis something of a moon, that beamed
  Upon her weak and trembling form,
And one beside, on whom she leaned,
  That scarce had stronger heart or arm—
Of souls united there until
  Death the last ties of life shall part,
And a fond kiss whose rapturous thrill
  Still vibrates softly in her heart.

It is an era strange, yet sweet,
  Which every woman's thought has known,
When first her young heart learns to beat
  To the soft music of a tone;
That era when she first begins
  To know what love alone can teach,
That there are hidden depths within
  Which friendship never yet could reach:
And all earth has of bitter wo
  Is light beside her hopeless doom

Who sees love's first sweet star below
  Fade slowly till it sets in gloom.
There may be heavier grief to move

When first her young heart learns to beat
  To the soft music of a tone.

  The heart that mourns an idol dead.
But one who weeps a living love
  Has surely little left to dread.

I cannot tell why love so true
  As theirs should only end in gloom;
Some mystery that I never knew
  Was woven darkly with their doom.
I only know their dream was vain,
  And that they woke to find it past,
And when by chance they met again,
  It was not as they parted last.
His was not faith that lightly dies,
  For truth and love as clearly shone
In the blue heaven of his soft eyes,
  As the dark midnight of her own:
And therefore Heaven alone can tell
  What are his living visions now;
But hers—the eye can read too well
  The language written on her brow.

In the soft twilight, dim and sweet,
  Once watching by the lattice pane,
She listened for his coming feet,
  For whom she never looked in vain:
Then hope shone brightly on her brow,
  That had not learned its after fears—
Alas! she cannot sit there now,
  But that her dark eyes fill with tears!
And every woodland pathway dim
  And bower of roses cool and sweet,
That speak of vanished days and him,
  Are spots forbidden to her feet.
No thought within her bosom stirs
  But wakes some feeling dark and dread:
God keep thee from a doom like hers—
  Of living when the hopes are dead!

THE FOLLOWERS OF CHRIST.

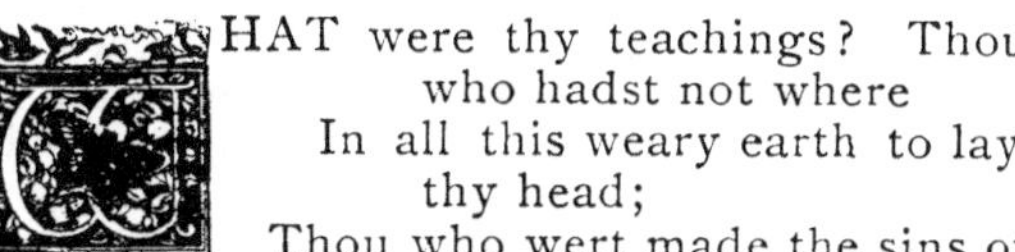

HAT were thy teachings? Thou
who hadst not where
In all this weary earth to lay
thy head;
Thou who wert made the sins of
men to bear,
And break with publicans thy daily bread!
Turning from Nazareth, the despised, aside,
And dwelling in the cities by the sea,
What were thy words to those who sat and
dried
Their nets upon the rocks of Galilee?

Didst thou not teach thy followers here
below,
Patience, long-suffering, charity, and love;
To be forgiving, and to anger slow,
And perfect, like our blessed Lord above?
And who were they, the called and chosen
then,
Through all the world, teaching thy truth,
to go?
Were they the rulers, and the chiefest men,
The teachers in the synagogue? Not so!
Makers of tents, and fishers by the sea,
These only left their all to follow thee.

And even of the twelve whom thou didst name
Apostles of thy holy word to be,
One was a devil; and the one who came
With loudest boasts of faith and constancy

He was the first thy warning who forgot,
And said, with curses, that he knew thee not!
Yet were there some who in thy sorrows were
  To thee even as a brother and a friend,
And women, seeking out the sepulchre,
  Were true and faithful even to the end:
And some there were who kept the living
      faith
Through persecution even unto death.

But, Saviour, since that dark and awful day
  When the dread temple's vail was rent in
      twain,
And while the noontide brightness fled away,
  The gaping earth gave up her dead again;
Tracing the many generations down,
  Who have professed to love thy holy ways,
Through the long centuries of the world's
      renown,
  And through the terrors of her darker
      days—
Where are thy followers, and what deeds of
      love
Their deep devotion to thy precepts prove?

Turn to the time when o'er the green hills
      came
  Peter the Hermit from the cloister's gloom,
Telling his followers in the Saviour's name
  To arm and battle for the sacred tomb;
Not with the Christian armor—perfect faith,
  And love which purifies the soul from
      dross—

But holding in one hand the sword of death,
And in the other lifting up the cross,
He roused the sleeping nations up to feel
All the blind ardor of unholy zeal!

With the bright banner of the cross unfurled,
And chanting sacred hymns, they marched, and yet
They made a pandemonium of the world,
More dark than that where fallen angels met:
The singing of their bugles could not drown
The bitter curses of the hunted down!
Richard, the lion-hearted, brave in war,
Tancred, and Godfrey, of the fearless band,
Though earthly fame had spread their names afar,
What were they but the scourges of the land?
And worse than these were men, whose touch would be
Pollution, vowed to lives of sanctity!

And in thy name did men in other days
Construct the Inquisition's gloomy cell,
And kindle persecution to a blaze,
Likest of all things to the fires of hell!
Ridley and Latimer—I hear their song
In calling up each martyr's glorious name,
And Cranmer, with the praises on his tongue
When his red hand dropped down amid the flame!

Merciful God! and have these things been
done,
And in the name of thy most holy Son?

Turning from other lands grown old in crime
To this, where Freedom's root is deeply set,
Surely no stain upon its folds sublime
Dims the escutcheon of our glory yet?

Hush! came there not a sound upon the air
Like captives moaning from their native
shore—
Woman's deep wail of passionate despair
For home and kindred seen on earth no
more!
Yes, standing in the market-place, I see
Our weaker brethren coldly bought and
sold,
To be in hopeless, dull captivity,
Driven forth to toil like cattle from the fold
And hark! the lash, and the despairing cry
Of the strong man in perilous agony!

And near me I can hear the heavy sound
Of the dull hammer borne upon the air:
Is a new city rising from the ground?
What hath the artisan constructed there?
'Tis not a palace, nor an humble shed;
'Tis not a holy temple reared by hands;
No!—lifting up its dark and bloody head
Right in the face of Heaven, the scaffold
stands;

And men, regardless of "Thou shalt not kill,"
  That plainest lesson in the Book of Light,
Even from the very altars tell us still
  That evil sanctioned by the law is right!
And preach in tones of eloquence sublime,
To teach mankind that murder is not crime!

And is there nothing to redeem mankind?
  No heart that keeps the love of God within?
Is the whole world degraded, weak, and blind,
  And darkened by the leprous scales of sin?
No, we will hope that some in meekness sweet,
Still sit, with trusting Mary, at thy feet.

For there are men of God, who faithful stand
  On the far ramparts of our Zion's wall,
Planting the cross of Jesus in some land
  That never listened to salvation's call.
And there are some, led by philanthropy,
  Men of the feeling heart and daring mind,
Who fain would set the hopeless captive free,
  And raise the weak and fallen of mankind.
And there are many in life's humblest way,
  Who tread like angels on a path of light,
Who warn the sinful when they go astray,
  And point the erring to the way of right;
And the meek beauty of such lives will teach
More than the eloquence of man can preach.

And, blessed Saviour! by thy life of trial,
  And by thy death, to free the world from sin,

And by the hope that man, though weak and vile,
  Hath something of divinity within—
Still will we trust, though sin and crime be met,
To see thy holy precepts triumph yet!

SONNETS.

I.

OWN in the cold and noiseless wave of death,
  Oh, pure and beautiful lost one that thou art,
Clasping the anchor of eternal faith
  Closer and closer to thy trusting heart—
Didst thou fade from us, while our tearful eyes,
  Here on the shore of sad mortality,
Gazed sorrowing on that form that ne'er shall rise
  Till sounds the music of eternity.
Then shalt thou take the Saviour's hand in thine,
  Not with his faith who held it falteringly,
But in the trustfulness of love divine,
  And with him walk the waters of the sea;
Till, casting anchor, all thy toils shall cease
In the still haven of eternal peace.

II.

THE beautiful measure of thy trusting love
Survives the answering faith it knew of old;
Over the heart thy pleadings cannot move,
Slowly, but sure, the closing wave hath rolled:
The unpitying eyes thou meet'st burn not more bright,
Though now thy lips with eloquent fervor speak,
And all thy passionate kisses may not light
The crimson fires in the unchanging cheek.
How shall I give thee solace? Had she died,
With love's sweet sunlight shining in her eyes,
Then might'st thou, casting selfish grief aside,
Patiently wait reunion in the skies:
For better than the living faith estranged,
The love that goes down to the dead unchanged.

III.

LOOK once again! yet morn in holy trust,
Near the still Presence softly, softly tread,
Before the dimness of the closing dust
Soils the yet lingering beauty of the dead.
Look on the silent lip, whence oft hath flowed
Such living truth as man hath seldom taught.

And the sereneness of that brow that glowed
Earnest in life with pure and eloquent thought!
How silver-white has grown his reverend hair,
Serving his Master in the way of truth:
For him, an age of active love and prayer
Fulfilled the beautiful promise of his youth;
And what a triumph houı is death to those
Faithful in life, yet happy in its close!

IV.

Let me not feel thy pitying finger's grasp,
Though dewy cool their pressure still may be,
Since they have learned to thrill within the clasp
Of passionate love that trembled once for me!
Sweep back the beautiful tresses from thy brow,
Nor let them, falling o'er me, blend with mine:
Dark as the glorious midnight in their flow,—
My locks are paler in their fall than thine!
In thy deep eyes are lit the fires divine,
That made the heart its early love forget;
So much they mock the softer light of mine
I cannot calmly meet their glances yet;
Therefore, until this bitterness shall cease,
Leave me, that I may win my heart to peace!

SYMPATHY.

N the same beaten channel still have run
The blessed streams of human sympathy;
And though I know this ever hath been done,
The why and wherefore I could never see:
Why some such sorrow for their griefs have won,
And some, unpitied, bear their misery,
Are mysteries, which thinking o'er and o'er
Has left me nothing wiser than before.

What bitter tears of agony have flowed
O'er the sad pages of some old romance!
How Beauty's cheek beneath those drops has glowed,
That dimmed the sparkling lustre of her glance,
And on some love-sick maiden is bestowed,
Or some rejected, hapless knight, perchance,
All her deep sympathies, until her moans
Stifle the nearer sound of living groans!

Oh, the deep sorrow for their suffering felt,
  Where is found something "better days" to prove!
What heart above their downfall will not melt,
  Who in a "higher circle" once could move!
For such, mankind have ever freely dealt
  Out the full measure of their pitying love,
Because they witnessed, in their wretchedness,
Their friends grow fewer and their fortunes less.

But for some humble peasant girl's distress,
  Some real being left to stem the tide,
Who saw her young heart's wealth of tenderness
  Betrayed, and trampled on, and flung aside—
Who seeks her out, to make her sorrows less?
  What noble lady o'er her tale hath cried?
None! for the records of such humble grief
Obtain not human pity—scarce belief.

And as for their distress, who from the first
  Have had no fortune and no friends to fail—
Those who in poverty were born and nursed—
  For such, by men, are placed without the pale
Of sympathy—since they are deemed the worst
  Who are the humblest, and if Want assail
And bring them harder toil, 'tis only said,
"They have been used to labor for their bread!"

Oh, the unknown, unpitied thousands found
Huddled together, hid from human sight
By fell disease or gnawing famine, bound
To some dim, crowded garret, day and night,
Or in unwholesome cellars underground,
With scarce a breath of air, or ray of light!
Hunger, and rags, and labor ill repaid—
These are the things that ask our tears and aid.

And these ought not to be; it is not well
Here in this land of Christian liberty,
That honest worth in hopeless want should dwell,
Unaided by our care and sympathy;
And is it not a burning shame to tell
We have no means to check such misery,
When wealth from out our treasury freely flows,
To wage a deadly warfare with our foes!

It is all wrong; yet men begin to deem
The days of darkest gloom are nearly done;
A something, like the first bright golden beam
That heralds in the coming of the dawn,
Breaks on the sight. Oh, if it be no dream,
How shall we haste that blessed era on!
For there is need that on men's hearts should fall
A spirit that shall sympathize with all.

MEMORIES.

"She loved me, but she left me."

EMORIES on memories! to my soul again
There come such dreams of vanished love and bliss,
That my wrung heart, though long inured to pain,
Sinks with the fulness of its wretchedness.
Thou dearer far than all the world beside!
Thou who didst listen to my love's first vow!
Once I had fondly hoped to call thee bride—
Is the dream over? comes the awakening now?
And is this hour of wretchedness and tears
The only guerdon for my wasted years?

And did I love thee; when by stealth we met
In the sweet evenings of that summer-time,
Whose pleasant memory lingers with me yet,
As the remembrance of a better clime
Might haunt a fallen angel. And oh! thou,
Thou who didst turn away and seek to bind
Thy heart from breaking, thou hast felt ere now
A heart like thine o'ermastereth the mind;
Affection's power is stronger than thy will;
Ah! thou didst love me, and thou lovest me still.

My heart could never yet be taught to move
With the calm even pulses that it should,
Turning away from those that it should love,
And loving whom it should not; it hath wooed
Beauty forbidden—I may not forget—
And thou, oh! thou canst never cease to feel;
But time, which hath not changed affection, yet
Hath taught at least one lesson—to conceal;
So none, but thou, who see my smiles shall know
The silent bleeding of the heart below.

MORALIZINGS.

HARK to the triumph for a victory won,
Shaking the solid earth whereon we stand!
What noble action hath the Nation done,
That thus rejoicing echoes through the land?
Hath she beheld life's inequality—
How, still, her stronger sons the weak oppress,
And, in the spirit of philanthropy,
Made the deep sum of human anguish less?
Or hath she risen up, at last to free
The hopeless slave from his captivity?

No, not for these the shout is heard to-night
  Waking its echoes in each vale and glen,
Not that the precepts of the Lord of Light
  Have found a dwelling in the hearts of
      men;
'Tis that a battle hath been fought and won,
  That the deep cannon's note is heard afar,
Telling us of the bloody conflict done,
  That Victory hovers o'er our ranks in war,
And that her soldiery their triumph sing
In the broad shadow of her starry wing.

And war is here! Impatient for the fight,
  Our Nation in her majesty arose,
Even as the restless lion in his might
  Up from the swelling of the Jordan goes,
And, with a trampling noise that shook each
      hill,
  On to the conflict madly hath she rushed,
Vowing to falter not, nor yield, until
  The life from out a Nation's heart is
      crushed;
Until her hapless sons are made to feel
The bloody vengeance of her iron heel!

And what will be our gain, though we return
  Proudly victorious from each battle plain?
A weakened Nation will be left to mourn
  Her bravest heroes in the conflict slain;
Her treasury drained; our broad and goodly
      land
  Filled with the orphan and the widowed
      wife;

A soldiery corrupted to disband,
Unfit for useful toil or virtuous life;
And a long train of evils yet to be
Darkly entailed upon posterity!

And this is glory! This is what hath been
To ages back the proudest theme of song,
And, dazzled by its glare, man has not seen
Beneath its pageantry the deadly wrong.
Deeming it fame to tread where heroes trod,
In his career he has not paused, or known
That all are children of the self-same God,
And that our brother's interest is our own;
For man that hardest lesson has to learn,
Still to forgive, and good for ill to return.

But oh! for all will come that solemn hour
When memory calls to mind each deed of sin,
And the world's hollow praise can have no power
To still the voice of conscious guilt within.
And grant, O Lord of Love, that it may be
My lot, when on the brink of death I press,
To think of some slight act of charity,
Some pang of human wretchedness made less,
So, that in numbering o'er life's deeds again,
I then may deem I have not lived in vain!

DREAMING OF HEAVEN.

I SIT where the shadows of twilight
steal o'er me,
While the wlidbirds are warb-
ling their last fitful hymn,
And I think of the loved who
have entered before me
That dwelling whose glory shall never
grow dim.

For ever the land of the spirits seems
nearer,
When twilight steals over the earth's quiet
breast,
And the harps of the angels sound sweeter
and clearer,
What time the last day-beams go out in the
west.

Oh! if all my dreams were as bright and
elysian
As those which the eve to my spirit still
brings,
I could sit here for ever to woo the sweet
vision,
And dream about heaven and heavenly
things!

For I long to be up where the seraphim
gather
With the ransomed of Zion whom Jesus has
blest,

And where, in the smile of our heavenly
Father,
Our purified spirits for ever shall rest!

MORNING THOUGHTS.

ROSSING the east with gold and crimson bars,
Comes the imperial King of day and light,
And, shaken by his tread, the burning stars
Drop from the regal diadem of night.
Surely the dawn was not more fair than this
When Eden's roses in fresh beauty burst,
And morning, blushing at her loveliness,
Looked down upon the young creation first:
When all below was innocent, and when
The angels walked in Paradise with man.

How equally the gifts of God come down
To all the creatures which his hand has made;
The beams that wake the children of renown,
Fall softly on the peasant in the glade.
The dawn that calls the eagle up to fly
From her proud eyrie to the mountain's height,
Visits the lowly lark as smilingly,
When from the vale she takes her homeward flight:

Morning and life and sunshine, these are things
That are not meant to be the wealth of kings!

Freedom at least from homeless poverty,
A soul unbowed by fetters or by pain,
One heart whose faith has still been true to me,
These things are mine, and why should I complain?
Complain! when God has been so good to me,
And when his blessings with my days increase,
Giving for every day of misery
A recompense of tranquil days of peace:
Even as the morning with her smiles and light
Is over-payment for the weary night.

THE MARINER'S BRIDE.

'ER the dark waters now my bounding bark
May bear me onward wheresoe'er it will:
I care not though the angry sky be dark,
Light of my being! thou art with me still.
Yes, let the heaving billows lash the deck,
And the red lightning tremble on the sea;
So that thy faithful arms are round my neck,
My heart will never tremble;—for with thee
I know my soul within would still be brave
If every gaping billow showed a grave.

Once I had feared the raging of the sea,
  When the wild tempest in its fury burst;
But, bride of beauty! standing thus with
    thee,
  The angry elements may do their worst.
And should our vessel founder on a rock,
  Or cast us on some desert shore to die,

Once I had feared the raging of the sea,
When the wild tempest in its fury burst.

Unshrinkingly my soul will meet the shock,
  If thou with that inspiring brow art nigh:
For, folding thee, my gentle bride, to sleep,
  Closer, and closer, to his fainting breast,

We should go down as calmly to the deep
As a youg infant to its cradle-rest.
And though the water-wraith should stir the sea,
  And the wild tempest move the waves above,
Securely peaceful would my slumber be
  With thee, my stricken bride of youth and love;
For thou wouldst cheer the darkness of the grave,
As the bright sea-star lights the ocean cave!

THE PRISONER'S LAST NIGHT.

HE last red gold had melted from the sky,
  Where the sweet sunset lingered soft and warm,
A starry night was gathering silently
  The jewelled mantle round her legal form;
While the invisible fingers of the breeze
Shook the young blossoms lightly from the trees.

Yet were there breaking hearts beneath the stars,
  Though the hushed earth lay smiling in the light,
And the dull fetters and the prison bars
  Saw bitter tears of agony that night,

And heard such burning words of love and truth
As wring the life-drops from the heart of youth.

For he, whom men relentless doomed to die,
Parted with one who loved him till the last;
With many a vow of faith and constancy
The long, long watches of the night were passed;
Till, heavily and slow, the prison door
Swung back, and told them that their hour was o'er.

'Twas his last night on earth! and God alone
Can tell the anguish of that stricken one,
Fettered in darkness to the dungeon stone,
And doomed to perish with the rising sun;
And she, whose faith through all was vainly true,
Her heart was broken—and she perished too!

And will this win an erring brother back
To the sweet paths of pleasantness and peace?
"While crimes are punished but by crime more black,"
Will sin, and wickedness, and sorrow cease?
No! crime will never cease to scourge the land,
So long as blood is on her ruler's hand!

And oh! how long will hearts in sin and pride
Reject his blessed precepts, who of yore

Taught men forgiveness on the mountain side,
  And spoke of love and mercy by the shore?
How long will power, with such despotic sway,
Trample unfriended weakness in its way?

Hasten, O Lord of Light, that glorious time,
  When man no more shall spurn thy wise
    command,
Filling the earth with wretchedness and crime,
  And making guilt a plague-spot on the
    land;
Hasten the time, that blood no more shall cry
Unceasingly for vengeance to the sky!

SONG OF THE HEART.

THEY may tell for ever of worlds of
    bloom
  Beyond the skies and beyond the
    tomb;
Of the sweet repose, and the rapture there,
That are not found in a world of care;
But not to me can the present seem
Like a foolish tale or an idle dream.

Oh, I know that the bowers of heaven are fair,
And I know that the waters of life are there;
But I do not long for their happy flow,
While there bursts such fountains of bliss
    below;
And I would not leave, for the rest above,
The faithful bosom of trusting love!

There are angels here; they are seen the while
In each love-lit brow and each gentle smile:
There are seraph voices, that meet the ear
In the kindly tone and the word of cheer;
And light, such light as they have above,
Beams on us here, from the eyes of love.

Yet, when it cometh my time to die,
I would turn from this bright world willingly;
Though, even then, would the thoughts of this
Tinge every dream of that land of bliss;
And I fain would lean on the loved for aid,
Nor walk alone through the vale and shade

And if 'tis mine, till life's changes end,
To keep the heart of one faithful friend,
Whatever the trials of earth may be,—
On the peaceful shore, or the restless sea,
In a palace home, or the wilderness,—
There is heaven for me in a world like this!

MAN BELIEVES THE STRONG.

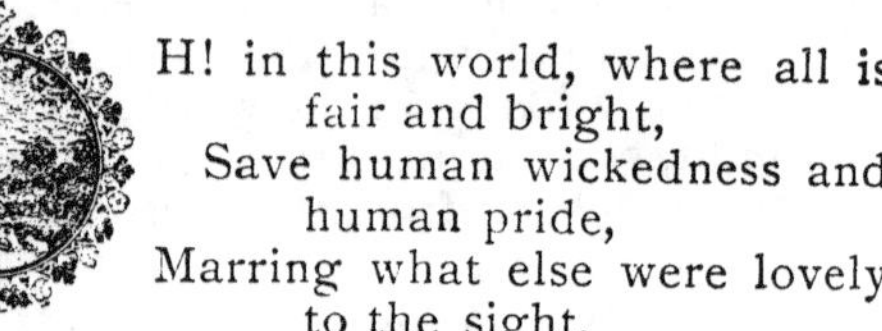
H! in this world, where all is fair and bright,
Save human wickedness and human pride,
Marring what else were lovely to the sight,
It is a truth that may not be denied,
However deeply we deplore the wrong,
Man hath believed, and still believes the strong.

When injured and defenceless woman stands,
Haply the child of innocence or youth,
And lifts to heaven her pleading voice and hands
In all the moving eloquence of truth,
Who will believe, in that most trying hour,
Her words who is not strong in wealth or power?

Or let the slave, of all on earth bereft,
Stand up to plead before a human bar;
And though the fetters and the lash have left
Upon his limbs the deep-attesting scar,
Who trusts his tale, or who will rise to save
From wrong and injury the outcast slave?

If a poor, friendless criminal appear,—
A criminal which men themselves have made,
By the injustice and oppression here,—

Who to pronounce him "*guilty*" is afraid?
But who, if rank or wealth were doomed
thereby,
Would speak that final word as fearlessly?

Oh, where so much of wrong and sorrow are,
There must be need of an unfaltering trust
In His all-seeing watchfulness and care,
Whose ways to man below we know are just;
In Him, whose love has numbered every tear
Wrung from his weak, defenceless creatures
here.

And there is need of earnest, full belief,
And patient work, to bring that holier day
When there shall be redress for humblest
grief,
And equal right and justice shall have sway;
And we will strive, in trustfulness sublime,
Hoping our eyes may see the blessed time!

THE HOMESICK PEASANT.

OH! I am sick of cities; all night
long
Orchards and corn-fields waved
before my sight,
Till the quick moving of the
restless throng
Broke on that pleasant vision of the night
With an unwelcome sound, and called my feet
Back from the meadows to the crowded
street.

I grew a child of Nature on the hills,
  Learning no lessons from the lips of Art,
And the restraint of cities cramps and chills

I grew a child of nature on the hills,
  Learning no lessons from the lips of Art.

  The warm, impulsive feelings of my heart;
Even the ceaseless stir and motion here
Grates with a jarring sound upon my ear.

It is not like my childhood: from the trees,
And from the flowers that grew beneath my feet,

And from the artless whispers of the breeze,
I never learned the lessons of deceit:
They never taught me that my heart should hide

Its thoughts and feelings with a mask of
pride.

And therefore with the morning I awake,
To feel a homesick yearning for the hills—
A thirst no water on the earth can slake,
Save the clear gushing of my native rills;
And I once more upon their banks would
stand,
Free as the breezes of my native land.

Give me a sweet home, set among the trees,
With friends whose words are ever kind
and true,
And books whose stories should instruct and
please,
When round the quiet hearth the household
drew;
For in their pleasant pages I can find
All I would learn of cities and mankind.

HOMES FOR ALL.

COLUMBIA, fairest nation of the
world,
Sitting in queenly beauty in the
west,
With all thy banners round about
thee furled,
Nursing the cherub Peace upon thy breast;
Never did daughter of a kingly line
Look on a lovelier heritage than thine!

Thou hast deep forests stretching far away,
The giant growth of the long centuries,
From whose dim shadows to the light of day
Come forth the mighty rivers toward the seas,
To walk like happy lovers, hand in hand,
Down through the green vales of our pleasant land.

Thou hast broad prairies, where the lovely flowers
Blossom and perish with the changing year;
Where harvests wave not through the summer hours,
Nor with the autumn ripen in the ear;
And beautiful lakes that toss their milky spray
Where the strong ship hath never cleaved its way.

And yet with all thy broad and fertile land,
Where hands sow not, nor gather in the grain,
Thy children come and round about thee stand,
Asking the blessing of a home in vain,—
Still lingering, but with feet that long to press
Through the green windings of the wilderness.

In populous cities do men live and die,
That never breathe the pure and liberal air;

Down where the damp and desolate rice-
swamps lie,
Wearying the ear of Heaven with constant
prayer,
Are souls that never yet have learned to raise
Under God's equal sky the psalm of praise.

Turn not, Columbia! from their pleading
eyes;
Give to thy sons that ask of thee a home;
So shall they gather round thee, not with
sighs,
But as young children to their mother
come;
And brightly to the centuries shall go down
The glory that thou wearest like a crown.

HARVEST GATHERING.

HE last days of the summer: bright
and clear
Shines the warm sun down on
the quiet land,
Where corn-fields, thick and heavy
in the ear,
Are slowly ripening for the laborer's hand;
Seed-time and harvest—since the bow was set,
Not vainly has man hoped your coming yet!

To the quick rush of sickles, joyously
The reapers in the yellow wheat-fields sung,

And bound the pale sheaves of the ripened
rye,
When the first tassels of the maize were
hung;
That precious seed into the furrow cast
Earliest in spring-time, crowns the harvest
last.

Ever, when summer's sun burns faint and
dim,
And rare and few the pleasant days are
given,
When the sweet praise of our thanksgiving
hymn
Makes beautiful music in the ear of Heaven,
I think of other harvests whence the sound
Of singing comes not as the sheaves are
bound.

Not where the rice-fields whiten in the sun,
And the warm South casts down her yellow
fruit,
Shout they the labors of the autumn done—
For there Oppression casts her deadly root,
And they, who sow and gather in that clime,
Share not the treasures of the harvest-time.

God of the seasons! thou who didst ordain
Bread for the eater who shall plant the soil,
How have they heard thee, who have forged
the chain
And built the dungeon for the sons of toil?

Burdening their hearts, not with the voice of
prayer,
But the dull cries of almost dumb despair.

They who would see that growth of wicked-
ness
Planted where now the peaceful prairie
waves,
And make the green paths of our wilderness
Red with the torn and bleeding feet of
slaves—
Forbid it, Heaven! and let the sharp axe be
Laid at the root of that most poison tree!

Let us behold its deadly leaves begin
A fainter shadow o'er the world to cast,
And the long day that nursed its growth of
sin
Wane to a sunset that shall be its last;
So that the day-star, rising from the sea,
Shall light a land whose children will be free!

PRAYER.

FATHER! thou didst hear my prayer,
When I plead with thee to spare,
When I asked for length of years,
Thou didst pitying see my tears,
And thy words in answer were,
"Respite from the sepulchre!"
Lo! no more the prayer I raise:

Life hath waned to evil days;
Veiling in the dust my woes,
I would bless the grave's repose;
Sweeter, sweeter would it be,
Than a lover's dream to me.

Long enough thy child hath been
Sruggling in a world of sin,
Long enough have doubts assailed,
Long enough the flesh prevailed,
Long enough hath sorrow tried
One it hath not purified.

In life's hours of rosy dawn,
Hope with white hand let me on,
Showing gorgeous imagery
Of a happier time to be;
But, in noonday's clearer flame,
Blest fruition never came.

Hastening now towards its close
Is the day that brightly rose,
And the hope that fled its prime
Comes not at the evening time,
Hear me, pity, and recall,
Ere the midnight shadows fall!

Willing, eager to depart,
Old in years and old in heart,
Waiting but the messenger
To unseal the sepulchre,
Lo! again to Thee I come—
Take me, Father, take me home!

LIFE IS NOT VANITY.

ARE ye not erring teachers
Who tell us, that below
There is no sparkling fountain
Where living waters flow;
That all earth's well-springs bubble up
With bitter drops of wo?
That life's a night of darkness,
With scarce a cheering star,—
That we cannot make our trials
Less bitter than tney are,—
That we should think of heaven alone,
And Heaven itself is far.

No marvel earth is dark to you
Who thus in shadows keep,—
That you cannot see the day-spring
When you close your eyes and sleep;
Or that earth is but a vale of tears
For you who sit and weep.

You tell us of the happiness
Of the unchanging sphere

Because the loved and loving there
  To bless us will be near;
If that be heaven, what hinders us
  To make a heaven here?

Oh, would we rouse from slumber,
  Life hath something to be done;
We may lose the prize by faltering,
  Which exertion might have won;
And when we strive to help ourselves,
  The Lord will aid us on.

And if we be immortal,
  As we believe and know,
Then is the life eternal
  Begun in life below;
And hath it been ordained by heaven,
  That it should be in wo?

No! and though trailing shadows
  O'er our pathway sometimes move,
Yet below, as in the life to come,
  All things are ruled in love,
And God will bless as willingly
  As he will do above!

And if we cheer life's marches,
  And smooth the path beneath,
If we labor for advancement
  With a true and earnest faith;
We shall stand prepared for lengthened years,
  Or for the call of death!

BURIAL HYMN.

EARTH to earth, and dust to dust:
Here, in calm and holy trust,
We have made her quiet bed
With the pale hosts of the dead,
And, with hearts that, stricken, weep,
Come to lay her down to sleep.

From life's weary cares set free,
Mother Earth, she comes to thee!
Hiding from its ills and storms
In the shelter of thine arms:
Peaceful, peaceful be her rest,
Here upon thy faithful breast.

And when sweetly from the dust
Heaven's last summons calls the just,
Saviour! when the nations rise
Up to meet thee in the skies,
Gently, gently, by the hand,
Lead her to the better land!

SONG OF THE REFORMED.

SEEKING its place of rest,
Each in its quiet nest,
All the glad warblers have hushed their last song;
And the first star of night,
With her faint silver light,
Guideth my homeward steps safely along.

Oh! to that quiet home,
With what delight I come,
When from the cares of the day I am free;
For with her happy smile,
There my young wife the while
Sits by the lattice pane watching for me.

But when I sought the board
Where the red wine is poured,
Oft has she fled when my footsteps drew near,
And nestling down to rest,
Close to that faithful breast,
Has my young infant turned from me in fear.

Silently then each day
Passed her sad life away—
Silently then was our sweet child caressed;
Now our low cabin rings
With the glad song she sings,
Rocking it nightly to sleep on her breast.

There I can see the light
Where our warm hearth is bright,
Oh! is there bliss more ecstatic above
Than this full heart can know,
Blest with your smiles below,
Wife of my bosom and child of my love?

THE COLD WATER ARMY.

IRMLY they still have stood,
A true and fearless band,
For the noble cause of human good
Hath nerved each heart and hand.
And they fear not the frowns of earth,
The mocking sneers of men,
For they fight for the sacred home and hearth,
For their trampled rights again.

In their ranks, no longer thin and weak,
Are men of every age,
From the stripling slight, with a beardless cheek,
To the silver-headed sage.
Oh, their hosts would darken the summer sea,
Were their banners all outspread,
And the dens of guilt rock tremblingly
With their firm and heavy tread.

They come not, an invading band,
With dreams of high renown,
To spoil the homes of our happy land,
And trample her vineyards down;
But to hunt that monster of sin and crime,
Which the slaves of the wine-cup know,
Who tracks his way in a path of slime
O'er the fairest flowers below.

For undisturbed has he roamed the earth
  Till his serpent brood have come
To nest themselves in the very hearth
  Of many a once bright home.
Yet, hearing the widow and orphan's sigh,
  And knowing he wounds to kill,
There are those so deaf to a nation's cry
  They would shield the monster still.

But our army follows with noiseless tread
  Wherever he winds his way,
As, feeling the bruise on his venomed head,
  He shrinks from the light of day;
And ne'er on the unsheathed sword and spear
  Will their hand relax its grasp,
Till they pause, and lean on their arms, to hear
  The sound of his dying gasp.

COMING HOME.

HOW long it seems since first we heard
  The cry of "Land in sight!"
Our vessel surely never sailed
  So slowly till to-night.
When we discerned the distant hills,
  The sun was scarcely set,
And now the noon of night is passed,
  They seem no nearer yet.

**Where the blue Rhine reflected back
Each frowning castle wall.**

Where the blue Rhine reflected back
  Each frowning castle wall,
Where, in the forest of the Hartz,
  Eternal shadows fall—
Or where the yellow Tiber flowed
  By the old hills of Rome,
I never felt such restlessness,
  Such longing for our home.

Dost thou remember, oh! my friend,
  When we beheld it last,
How shadows from the setting sun
  Upon our cot were cast?
Three summer-times upon its walls
  Have shone for us in vain;
But, oh! we're hastening homeward now,
  To leave it not again.

There, as the last star dropped away,
  From Night's imperial brow,
Did not our vessel "round thè point?"
  The land looks nearer now!
Yes, as the first faint beams of day
  Fall on our native shore,
They're dropping anchor in the bay—
  We're home, we're home once more!

PARTING AND MEETING.

N the casement, closed and
    lonesome,
  Is falling the autumn rain,
And my heart to-night is heavy
  With a sense of unquiet pain.

Not that the leaves are dying
  In the kiss of the traitor frost,
And not that the summer flowers
  On the bitter winds are tossed.

And not that the reaper's singing
The time no longer cheers,
Bringing home through the mellow starlight
The sheaves and the yellow ears.

No, not from these am I sighing,
As the hours pass slow and dull,
For God in his own time maketh
All seasons beautiful.

But one of our household number
Sits not by the hearth-fire's light,
And right on her pathway beating
Is the rain of this autumn night.

And therefore my heart is heavy
With a sense of unquiet pain,
For, but Heaven can tell if the parted
Shall meet in the earth again.

But knowing God's love extendeth
Wherever his children are,
And tenderly round about them
Are the arms of his watchful care;

With him be the time and the season
Of our meeting again with thee,
Whether here on these earthly borders,
Or the shore of the world to be.

THE REEFER.

YES, sailor, when the angry deep
Its war with heaven is waging,
I'll tell thee why I sit and weep
When thus the storm is raging.
Once when the sea, as now, was tossed
With fierce and wild commotion,
I stood unheeding on the coast,
And watched the troubled ocean.

For as the arrowy bolts were hurled
In fiery wrath from heaven,
We saw afar, with canvas furled,
A ship through darkness driven.
I had a brother then, whose bark
Upon the sea was riding,
And when I saw that vessel dark,
I knew his hand was guiding.

And now, as fiercer came the light,
And as the storm grew drearer,
We saw her through the gathering night
Come near the strand, and nearer!
Already fancy clasped once more
The form so fondly cherished,
When, reaching to the fatal shore,
That vessel struck and perished!

And now, upon the sea, when'er
The black clouds o'er us hover,

I see that frail bark strike, and hear
  The shriek that rose above her!
No change can lull my thoughts to sleep,
  No time my grief assuages;
And therefore, sailor, do I weep,
  When thus the tempest rages.

A TIME TO DIE.

LIKE the music deep and solemn
    In some ruined church,
  Floating over crumbling column
    And fallen arch;
  Through the naked branches trailing
    Low on the ground,
Come the winds of autumn wailing
    With a ghostly sound.

Over all below a feeling
    Of quiet reigns,
Like a drowsy numbness stealing
    Through the veins.
Even the sun, in the dim haze mourning,
    Hides his head,
Like a sickly taper burning
    Beside the dead.

And all day one feeling busy
    In my soul hath wrought,

Till heart and brain are dizzy
With the solemn thought.
In the shadow of deep dejection
I sit and sigh,
With but one sad reflection,
"A TIME TO DIE!"

O God of the soul immortal!
If death be near,
Teach me to tread that portal
And not to fear.
Keep thou my feet from turning
Aside to die;
Let my lamp be filled and burning
For the "MIDNIGHT CRY!"

LOVE AT THE GRAVE.

EMEMBRANCER of nature's prime,
And herald of her fading near,
The last month of the summer time
Of leaves and flowers is with us here

More eloquent than lip can preach
To every heart that hopes and fears
What solemn lessons does it teach
Of the quick passage of our years!

To me it brings sad thoughts of one,
Who, in the summer's fading bloom,
Bright from the arms of love went down
To the dim silence of the tomb.

How often since has spring's soft shower
Revived the life in nature's breast,
And the sweet herb and tender flower
Have been renewed above her rest!

How many summer times have told
To mortal hearts their rapid flight,
Since first this heap of yellow mould
Shut out her beauty from my sight;

Since first, to love's sweet promise true,
My feet beside her pillow trod,
Till year by year the pathway grew
Deeper and deeper in the sod!

Now these neglected roses tell
Of no kind hand to tend them nigh;
Oh, God! I have not kept so well
My faith as in the years gone by.

But here to-day my step returns,
And, kneeling where these willows wave,
As the soft flame of sunrise burns
Down through the dim leaves to thy grave

I cry, Forgive that I should prove
  Forgetful of thy memory;
Forgive me, that a living love
  Once came between my soul and thee!

For the weak heart that faintly yearned
  For human love its life to cheer,
Baffled and bleeding has returned
  To stifle down its crying here.

For, steadfast still, thy faith to me
  Was one which earth could not estrange:
And, lost one! where the angels be
  I know affection may not change.

STRENGTH OF SIN.

NOW lately and this beautiful earth
  was shut by darkness from my sight,
And all the mighty arch of blue
  Was sparkling with its worlds of light.

Waning and waning, one by one
  They vanished as the day-star rose,
Till, lo? along the distant hills
  The fire of sunrise burns and glows

And turning from the hosts of heaven
  To the calm beauty of the earth,
I feel what goodness must be his
  Who spoke his glories into birth.

More than our hearts can comprehend,
  Or our weak, blinded eyes can see,
The wisdom and the love of God,
  How mighty and how vast they be.

Too fair for us to hate or leave
  This world his hand has placed us in,
But for the presence and the power
  Of that most fiery serpent, sin—

That first in Eden's peaceful shade
  Uncoiled its bright and deadly folds,
And living still, and unsubdued,
  Sends its dark poison through our souls

But from his creatures blind and lost,
  God never wholly turned aside,
As power to save us from the curse
  Was sent us when the Saviour died.

All that is left us under heaven,
  Hope of the lost and sin-enslaved,
The only Name on earth that's given,
  Whereby the souls of men are saved.

Thanks unto God, that he was sent
  A sacred warfare to begin,
That in the end shall surely crush
  And bind the infernal strength of sin!

That by him it shall be at last
  Out from this fair creation hurled,
Who gave its death-blow when the cross
  Was darkly planted in the world.

And thanks to Him, that when the soul
  In agony for mercy calls,
Right in the shadow of that cross
  The sunlight of his pardon falls.

THE PLACE OF GRAVES.

HOW often in the summers gone,
  I've stood where these memorials rise,
And every time the spot had grown
  Less and less lonely to mine eyes.

The first I ever loved that died
  Sleeps here, where these sweet roses wave;
A maiden, with life's path untried,
  She left the sunshine for the grave.

And what a place of desolate gloom
  Seemed then to me the realm of death,
Though she I loved went calmly down,
  In all the truthfulness of faith.

The next, a sweet lamb of the fold,
  An infant, lulled to slumber lay,
With her pale locks of finest gold
  Put softly from her brow away.

But when the patient mother prest
  To her meek lips the bitter cup,
And came with those she loved to rest,
  Till God shall call the sleepers up,

Then the dim pathway grew more clear,
  That leads through darkness to the light,
And death has never seemed so drear,
  Nor heaven so distant from my sight.

FEARS.

OLD me closer to thy bosom,
  Let me feel thy clasping hand;
Wilder grows the night, and dreearer—
  Shall we never reach the land?

Thrice from dreams of broken slumber
  Have I started in affright;

On the shore I never trembled
  As I tremble here to-night.

Nay, 'tis not the haunting beauty
  Of some lovely vision gone—
But the watches wear so heavy;
  Leave me, leave me not alone!

Yes, I know the waves are calmer,
  And the sky has lost its frown,
But the sharp reefs, ere the morning
  We may strike them, and go down!

Said you that the dawn is breaking,
  With its gray uncertain light?
Look! I dare not trust my vision—
  Are the cliffs of home in sight?

Hush! I cannot, listening eager,
  Hear the heavy billows roar;
We are standing in still water—
  We are nearing to the shore!

Yes, above us, streaming seaward,
  Shine the red lights of the tower;
We are anchored—we are mooring—
  God be praised for such an hour!

MELODY.

THE beautiful eve, in her sparkling tiara,
With dew-dropping fingers is closing the flower,
Where thou, oh! my white-bosomed bird of the prairie,
Art watching and waiting for me in our bower.

My heart, beating quick as the pulse of the ocean,
Outstrips e'en my courser, to see thee again;
Though his limbs are as lithe and as fleet in their motion
As the barb in the desert, or roe on the plain.

My heart feels no presage of evil or danger,
For thou never wouldst fly, lovely warbler, from me:

And I hid thee so well that the spoiler and stranger
Could track not the windings which lead me to thee.

Yet faster, my steed: for the starlight discloses
Our bower, but no minstrel its shadows among;—
Yes, something is fluttering like wings in the roses,
And, bird of my bosom! I hear thy sweet song.

THE WOMEN AT THE SEPULCHRE.

MORN broke on Calvary, and the sun was flinging
The earliest brightness from his locks abroad,
As the meek sisters came in sadness, bringing
Gifts of sweet spices to anoint their Lord.

They who had loved his blessed precepts ever,
And linger'd with him when the earth was gloom,
They were the faithful who reviled him never,
"Last at the cross, and earliest at the tomb!"

I've sometimes thought I never could inherit
  A glorious mansion in the skies above:
For, oh! how weak and faltering is my spirit,
  Compared with such undying faith and love!

But, Father, can not all that heavenly meekness,
  That deathless love which all things could endure,
Can it not plead before Thee, for the weakness
  Of one whose faith is oft so faint and poor?

THE WATCHER.

'TIS the third summer that has gone,
  Since first upon that sloping hill,
He listened for the feet of one
  Whose coming he is waiting still.

All through the evenings warm and bland,
  When the red sunset lights the skies,
Then first we see the watcher stand,
  With hope reflected in his eyes:

Still waiting through the tranquil hours,
  Till eve with fingers, fair and slight,
Has folded up to sleep the flowers,
  And left them with the peaceful night.

But when the stars like fire-sparks glow
  In the far pavement of the sky,
Then hope, that lingered on till now,
  Fades slowly from his cheek and eye.

And when the still night, wearing on,
  Has almost broken into day,
As if he knew she would not come,
  He turns with mournful step away.

Oh, heavily, and dull, and slow,
  Such hours of anxious vigil wane:
God keep that watcher in his wo,
  Who looks for coming feet in vain.

'Twas on the morning of a day
  Sweet as the night-time ever nursed,
Her white arms filled with flowers of May,
  He saw the village maiden first.

Like the last hues of dying day,
  Which sunset from his path has rolled,
The roses of the summer lay
  Softly among her locks of gold.

Singing a soft and plaintive lay,
  She won him with her gentle tone,
And then he stole her heart away
  With voice as witching as her own.

And once, when the sweet stars as now
  Look calmly down upon that hill,
Their young hearts breathed the tender vow
  Which one has kept so faithful still.

And meeting nightly, 'twas not strange,
But yet he dreamed not love could wane,
Or thought that human hearts might change,
Until he waited there in vain.

And still, to meet her on that height,
He lingers as in summers gone,
Till evening deepening into night,
He wakes to find himself alone.

For none till now have ever told
That watcher of expectant hours,
How long ago her locks of gold
Were braided with the bridal flowers.

CHALMERS.

IN the hush of the desolate mid-night,
Leaving no brighter behind,
A noble light was stricken
From the galaxy of mind.

As the red lights down in the water,
When a boat shoots into the sea,
Or a star through the thin blue ether,
He vanished silently.

Not the counsel of ghostly fathers
Showed him the way he trod,
Not the picture of saints and martyrs,
Nor the smile of the Mother of God;

Not the love-lighted brows of kindred,
  Nor the words of a faithful friend,
Opened up the way to his vision,
  And cheered him to the end.

As a God-fearing man, and holy,
  He had passed through the snares beneath
And he needed no aid to strengthen
  His soul in the hour of death.

The steps of his faith were planted
  Where the waves in vain might beat,
While the waters of death rose darkly,
  And closed around his feet.

Not the "Save, or I perish!" of Peter,
  Was his as he faintly trod,
But the trust of that first blest martyr,
  Falling asleep in God.

And we may not mourn the brightness
  That is taken from our sky,
Which shall teach to the unborn ages
  The way to live and die.

SONG.

THE first and loveliest star of even
Shines on me with its first sweet light:
O thou, to whom my heart is given
What visions haunt thy soul to-night?

Dost thou, as this soft twilight steals
So mildly over hill and plain,
Think of the hour we parted last,
And wish me by thy side again?

I ask not that thy love should be
As deep, as trusting as my own,
I do not ask that thou shouldst feel
All that my woman's heart has known:

But if, for every thousand times
My spirit fondly turns to thee,
One thought of thine to me is given,
I doubt not thy fidelity.

For me, when on the hills alone,
Or treading through the noisy mart,
There is no time, there is no place,
But thou art with me in my heart.

I only think upon the past,
Or dream of happier days to be,
And every hope and every fear
Is something hoped or feared for thee.

THE ILLS OF LIFE.

HOW oft, when pursued by evils,
We falter and faint by the way,
But are fearless when, o'ertaken,
We pause, and turn at bay.

When storms in the distance have gathered,
I have trembled their wrath to meet,
Yet stood firm when the arrowy lightning
Has fallen at my feet.

My soul in the shadows of twilight
Has groaned beneath its load,
And felt at the solemn midnight
Secure in the hand of God.

I have been with friends who were cherished
All earthly things above,
Till I deemed the death-pangs lighter
Than the pangs of parting love.

Yet with one fearful struggle,
When at last the dread blow fell,
I have kept my heart from breaking,
And calmly said, Farewell!

I have looked at the grave, and shuddered
For my kindred treading near,
And when their feet had entered,
My soul forgot its fear.

Our ills are not so many
  Nor so hard to bear below,
But our suffering in dread of the future
  Is more than our present wo.

We see with our vision imperfect
  Such causes of doubt and fear—
Some yet that are far in the distance,
  And some that may never be near—

When, if we would trust in his wisdom
  Whose purpose we may not see,
We would find, whatever our trials,
  As our day our strength shall be.

THE BRIDE.

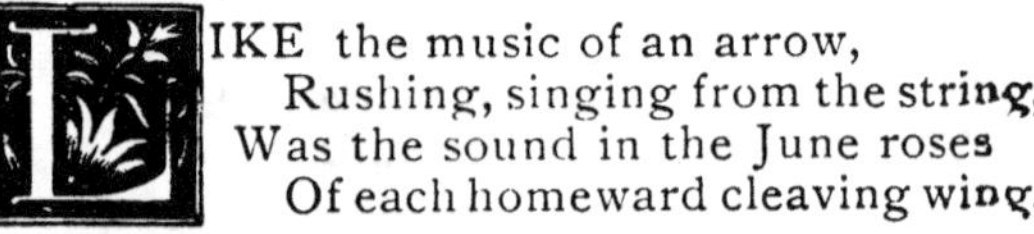

IKE the music of an arrow,
  Rushing, singing from the string,
Was the sound in the June roses
  Of each homeward cleaving wing,

Where the leaves were softly parted
  By a hand of snowy grace,
Letting in a shower of sunlight
  Brightly o'er an eager face;

O'er the young face of a maiden,
  Touched by changing hope and fear,
As the sound of rapid hoof-strokes,
  Nearing, fell upon the ear.

White robes softly heaving, fluttering,
  O'er her bosom's rise of snow,
Spoke the strange and soft confession
  Of the beating heart below.

And the face had sweet revealings,
  Sweeter than the lip may speak,
For the soft fires of confession
  Lit their crimson in the cheek.

Not for friend, and not for brother,
  Kept she eager vigil there;
Not for friend, and not for brother,
  Gleamed the roses in her hair.

. . . .

Myriad frost-sparks fire-like glittered
  In the keen and bitter air,
And no wild bird, dropping downward,
  Stirred the branches cold and bare.

Flaming in the glorious forehead
  Of the midnight, high and lone,
Starry constellations, steadfast,
  Yet like burning jewels shone;

When, from a sick couch uplifted,
  A thin hand, most snowy white,
Parted back the curtains softly,
  Letting in the pallid light.

Eyes of more than mortal brightness
  Spoke the waiting heart's desire,
And the hollow cheeks were lighted
  With a quick, consuming fire.

That young watcher in the roses,
  Of the earnest eye and brow,
Keeps again her anxious vigil;
  Who shall end its moments now?

Lo! the breast is softly trembling,
  But with hope that has no fear:
By that happy smile the Presence
  She hath waited for is near!

For a bridegroom hath she tarried;
  Bring the roses for her brow;
Though no human passion answers
  To his icy kisses now.

Bride of earth! here, hoping, fearing,
  Evil were thy days, and vain;
Bride of heaven! for blest fruition
  Thou shalt never wait again.

REMEMBRANCE.

HAVE struggled long with weakness,
  But my heart is free at last;
Never more will it be haunted
  With the phantoms of the past.

Never more, from fairest maiden,
  The light witchery of a word
Shall thrill my heart with rapture,
  When its magic tones are heard.

And that heart, so long made heavy
  With inquietude and wo,
From its fetters loosed, is ringing,
  Like a quick shaft from the bow.

Forgotten be the trusted
  That have lightly broke their trust;
And the dreams that I have cherished,
  Let them perish in the dust.

Yet there was one fair maiden,
  Sweetest vision of my youth,
She was lovely when I loved her,
  And her words were like the truth.

And they may have torn her from me;
  She was faithful once, I know—
No, she smiled beside the altar,
  And 'twas not to hide her wo!

And how can she, smiling, meet me
  With that fearless, open brow?
'Twas like heaven, of old, to kiss it,
  'Twould be heaven to kiss it now.

Pause, remembrance, since forever,
  Leila, dreams of thee are sin—
Oh, I thought my heart was stronger!
  Till I paused and looked within.

ENTERING HEAVEN.

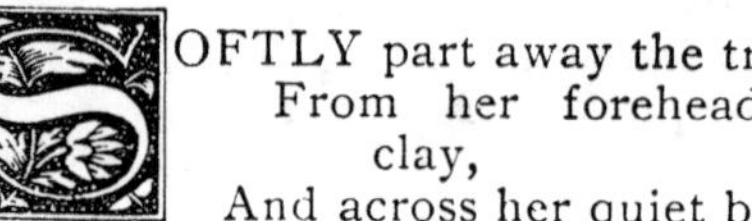

SOFTLY part away the tresses
From her forehead of white clay,
And across her quiet bosom
Let her pale hands lightly lay;
Never idly in her lifetime
Were they folded thus away.

She hath lived a life of labor,
She has done with toil and care,
She hath lived a life of sorrow,
She has nothing more to bear,
And the lips that never murmured
Never more shall move in prayer.

You who watched with me beside her,
As her last of nights went by,
Know how calmly she assured us
That her hour was drawing nigh;
How she told us, sweetly smiling,
She was glad that she could die.

Many times from off the pillow
Lifting up her face to hear,
She had seemed to watch and listen,
Half in hope and half in fear,
Often asking those about her
If the day were drawing near.

Till at last, as one aweary,
To herself she murmured low,

"Could I see him, could I bless him
  Only once before I go;
If he knew that I was dying,
  He would come to me, I know."

Drawing, then, my head down gently,
  Till it lay beside her own,
Said she, "Tell him in his anguish,
  When he finds that I am gone,
That the bitterness of dying
  Was to leave him here alone.

"Leave me now, my dear ones, leave me,
  You are wearied now, I know;
You have all been kind and watchful,
  You can do no more below,
And if none I love are near me,
  'Twill be easier to go.

"Let your warm hands chill not slipping
  From my fingers' icy tips,
Be there not the touch of kisses
  On my uncaressing lips,
Let no kindness see the darkening
  Of my eyes' last, long eclipse.

"Never think of me as lying
  By the dismal mould o'erspread,
But about the soft white pillow
  Folded underneath my head;
And of summer flowers weaving
  A rich broidery o'er my bed.

"Think of the immortal spirit
  Living up above the sky,
And of how my face, there wearing
  Light of immortality,
Looking earthward, is o'erleaning
  The white bastions of the sky."

Stilling, then, with one last effort,
  All her weakness and her wo,
She seemed wrapt in pleasant visions
  But to wait her time to go;
For she never after midnight
  Spoke of anything below,—

But kept murmuring very softly
  Of cool streams and pleasant bowers,
Of a pathway going up brightly,
  Where the fields were white with flowers;
And at daybreak she had entered
  On a better life than ours.

OUR BABY.

WHEN the morning, half in shadow,
  Ran along the hill and meadow,
  And with milk-white fingers parted
  Crimson roses, golden-hearted;
Opening over ruins hoary
Every purple morning-glory,

And out shaking from the bushes
Singing larks and pleasant thrushes;—
That's the time our little baby,

Our Baby.

Strayed from Paradise, it may be,
Came with eyes like heaven above her
O, we could not choose but love her!

Not enough of earth for sinning,
Always gentle, always winning,
Never needing our reproving,
Ever lovely, ever loving;
Starry eyes and sunset tresses,
White arms, made for light caresses,
Lips that knew no word of doubting,
Often kissing, never pouting;
Beauty even in completeness,
Overfull in childish sweetness;—
That's the way our little baby,
Far too pure for earth, it may be,
Seemed to us, who while about her
Deemed we could not do without her.

When the morning, half in shadow,
Ran along the hill and meadow,
And with milk-white fingers parted
Crimson roses, golden-hearted;
Opening over ruins hoary
Every purple morning-glory,
And outshaking from the bushes
Singing larks and pleasant thrushes;—
That's the time our little baby,
Pining here for heaven, it may be,
Turning from our bitter weeping,
Closed her eyes as when in sleeping,
And her white hands on her bosom
Folded like a summer blossom.

Now the litter she doth lie on,
Strew with roses, bear to Zion;
Go, as past a pleasant meadow

Through the valley of the shadow;
Take her softly, holy angels,
Past the ranks of God's evangels,
Past the saints and martyrs holy,
To the Earth-born, meek and lowly;
We would have our precious blossom
Softly laid in Jesus' bosom.

THE OUTCAST.

HE died at the middle of night:
And brother nor sister, lover nor friend,
Came not near her their aid to lend,
Ere the spirit took its flight.

She died at the middle of night:
Food and raiment she had no more,
And the fire had died on the hearth before,—
'Twas a pitiful, pitiful sight.

She died at the middle of night:
No napkin pressed back the parted lips;
No weeper, watching the eyes' eclipse,
Covered them up from sight.

She died at the middle of night:
And there was no taper beside the dead,
But the stars, through the broken roof o'er-head,
Shone with a solemn light.

She died at the middle of night:
And the winter snow spread a winding-sheet
Over the body from head to feet,
Dainty, and soft, and white.

She died at the middle of night:
But if she heard, ere her hour was o'er,
"I have not condemned thee,—sin no more,"
She lives where the day is bright.

AT THE WATER'S EDGE.

HERE are little innocent ones,
And their love is wondrous strong
Clinging about her neck,
But they may not keep her long.

Father! give her strength
To loosen their grasp apart,
And to fold her empty hands
Calmly over her heart.

And if the mists of doubt
Fearfully rise and climb
Up from that river that rolls
Close by the shore of time,—

Suddenly rend it away,
Holy and Merciful One!

As the veil of the temple was rent,
  When the mission of Christ was done.

So she can see the clime
  Where the jasper walls begin,
And the pearl gates, half unclosed,
  Ready to shut her in.

So she can see the saints,
  As they beckon with shining hand,
Leaning over the towers,
  Waiting to see her land.

Saviour! we wait thy aid,
  For our human aid were vain;
We have gone to the water's edge,
  And must turn to the world again.

For she stands where the waves of death
  Fearfully surge and beat,
And the rock of the shore of life
  Is shelving under her feet.

OUR FRIEND.

WE tried to win her from her grief,
  To soothe her great despair;
We showed her how the starry flowers
  Were growing everywhere,—
The starry flowers she used to braid
  At evening in her hair.

We told her how our hearts, for her,
  Beat mournfully and low;
How lines were deepening, day by day,
  Across her father's brow;
And how her little brother drooped,—
  He had no playmate now.

And then she spoke of weary nights
  Of dull and sleepless pain,
And how she grieved that loving friends
  Should plead with her in vain;
And hoped that when the summer came
  She should be well again.

Still softly singing to herself
  Sad words of plaintive rhyme,
She always watched the sun's soft glow
  Fade off at eventime,
As one who nursed a pleasant dream
  Of some delicious clime.

Thus, sweetly as the flowers that once
  She wore at eventide,
Faded and drooped the gentle girl,
  A blossom by our side,
And her young light of life went out
  With sunset, when she died!

CHANGES.

NDER the evening splendor
Of spring's sweet skies,
Learned I love's lesson tender,
From the maiden's eyes.

When the stars, like lovers meeting,
In the blue appeared,
And my heart, tumultuous and beating,
Hoped and feared,—

Then the passion, long dissembled,
My lip made known,
And the hand of the maiden trembled
In my own,—

Till the tears that gushed unbidden,
Unrepressed,
And the crimson blush were hidden
On my breast.

And there in that vale elysian,
    Through the summer bland,
We walked in a tranced vision,
    Hand in hand.

There the evening shadows found us
    Side by side,
While the glorious roses round us
    Bloomed and died.

And when the bright sun waning,
    Dimly burned,—
When the wind with sad complaining,
    In the valley mourned,—

When the bridal roses faded
    In her hair,
And her brow was sweetly shaded
    With a thought of care,—

Then with heart still fondly thrilling,
    But with calmer bliss,
From the lip no more unwilling
    I claimed the kiss.

Then our dreams, with love o'erladen,
    Were verified,
And dearer to me than the maiden
    Grew the bride.

But when the dead leaves drifted
In that valley low,
And down from the cold sky sifted
The noiseless snow,—

Then our dreams, with love o'erladen,
Were verified.

Where the hearts of the faithful moulder
With the dead,
They made her a pillow colder
Than the bridal bed.

And there at the spring's returning,
With the summer's glow,
When the autumn sun is burning,
In the winter's snow,—

With the ghosts of the dim past ever
Gliding round,
Walk I in that vale, as a river
That makes no sound.

THE CONVICT'S CHILD.

NLOCK the still home of the dead,
Down to its slumber we would lay
One, who, with firm, unshrinking tread,
Drew near and nearer day by day.

For when the morn of life for her
Hid all its beautiful light in tears,
The shadow of the sepulchre
Woke in her soul no human fears.

Even in the spring-time of her youth,
Before that she had wept or striven,
With all its wealth of love and truth,
She gave her young heart up to heaven.

Something prophetic of her doom
  Before her vision sadly rose;
So, ere the evil days had come,
  She gathered strength to meet their woes

Child of a lost and guilty sire,
  She felt, what time must darkly prove,
That home and hearth were not for her,
  Nor the sweet ministries of love.

And when her trembling heart at last
  By maiden hopes and fears was thrilled.
Clasping the sacred cross more fast,
  That pleading for the earth was stilled.

Turning from eyes whose tender ray
  Burned with affection true and deep,
Love's passionate kisses never lay
  Upon her forehead but in sleep.

Yet more than mortal may be tried
  Was she who firmly bore that part,
And the meek martyr slowly died
  In crushing down the human heart.

Pitying in such a world of storms
  The woes of that unsheltered breast,
Death kindly took her in his arms,
  And rocked her to eternal rest.

Then softly, softly, down to sleep,
  Lay her where these white blossoms grow,
And where the Sabbath silence deep
  Is broken by no sound of woe;—

Where near her, the long summer through,
  Will sing this gently lulling stream;
'Tis the first rest she ever knew
  Haunted by no unquiet dream.

THE LIFE OF TRIAL.

AM glad her life is over,
  Glad that all her trials are past;
For her pillow was not softened
  Down with roses to the last.

When sharp thorns choked up the pathway
  Where she wandered sad and worn,
Never kind hand pressed them backward,
  So her feet were pierced and torn.

And when life's stern course of duty
  Through the fiery furnace ran,
Never saw she one beside her,
  Like unto the Son of Man.

Ere the holy dew of baptism
  Cooled her aching forehead's heat,
Heaviest waters of affliction
  Many times had touched her feet.

Long for her deliverance waiting,
  Clung she to the cross in vain;
With an agonizing birth-cry
  Was her spirit born again.

And her path grew always rougher,
  Wearier, wearier, still she trod,
Till, through gates of awful anguish,
  She went in at last to God!

DEATH OF A FRIEND.

HERE leaves by bitter winds are heaped
In the deep hollows, damp and cold,
And the light snow-shower, silently,
Is falling on the yellow mould,

Sleeps one who was our friend, below;—
With meek hands folded on her breast,
When the first flowers of summer died,
We softly laid her down to rest.

By her were blessings freely strewn,
As roses by the summer's breath;
Yet nothing in her perfect life
Was half so lovely as her death.

In the meek beauty of a faith
Which few have ever proved like her,
She shrunk not even when she felt
The chill breath of the sepulchre.

Heavier, and heavier still, she leaned
Upon his arm who died to save,
As step by step he led her down
To the still chamber of the grave.

'T was at the midnight's solemn watch
  She sunk to slumber, calm and deep:
The golden fingers of the dawn
  Shall never wake her from that sleep.

From him who was her friend below,
  She turned to meet her Heavenly Guide;
And the sweet children of her love,
  She left them sleeping when she died.

Her last of suns went calmly down,
  And when the morn rose bright and clear,
Hers was a holier Sabbath-day
  Than that which dawned upon us here.

DEATH SCENE.

YING, still slowly dying,
  As the hours of night wore by,
She had lain since the light of sunset
  Was red on the evening sky,—

Till after the middle watches,
  As we softly near her trod,
When her soul from its prison fetters
  Was loosed by the hand of God.

One moment her pale lips trembled
  With the triumph she might not tell,
As the light of the life immortal
  On her spirit's vision fell.

Then the look of rapture faded,
  And the beautiful smile waxed faint,
As that in some convent picture
  On the face of a dying saint.

And we felt in the lonesome midnight,
  As we sat by the silent dead,
What a light on the path going downward
  The steps of the righteous shed;—

When we thought how with feet unshrinking
  She came to the Jordan's tide,
And, taking the hand of the Saviour,
  Went up on the heavenly side!

DEAD.

DEAD! yet there comes no shriek, on tear,—
  My agony is dumb;
I've thought, and feared, and known so long
  That such an hour must come:

For when her once sweet household cares
  Grew wearier every day,
And, dropping from her listless hand,
  Her work was put away.

I knew that all her tasks were done,
  And, though I wept and prayed,
I always thought of her as one
  For whom the shroud is made.

She talked of growing strong and well,
  To soothe our parting pain:
I knew it would be well with her
  Before we met again;—

I knew upon that lonesome hill,
  Where winter now is drear,
They'd have to make another grave
  Before another year.

I hope that they will dig it there:
  I would not have it made
Between the graves where strangers sleep,
  Under the cypress shade.

I'd have it where our sisters gone
  Are sleeping side by side,
And where we weeping orphans laid
  Our mother when she died.

There, too, with beauty scarcely dimmed,
  And curls of shining gold,
We covered little Ellie's face,
  And hid it in the mould.

So bring her there, and when they rise
  Who in the dust have lain,
She'll see her little baby wake,
  And take him up again.

THE WATCHER'S STORY.

SHE has slept since first the firelight
Mingled with the sun's last ray,—
If she lives till after midnight
She may see another day;—
Though she then could only number
A few weary hours, at best,
And 't were better if her slumbe
Could be deepened into rest

When about my neck, all night through.
White arms. softly dimpled, lay,
Then her face had not a shadow
That I could not kiss away:
And I knew the simple measure
Of her little hopes and fears,
Shared in all her childish pleasure,
Pitied all her childish fears.

But the maiden's deeper yearning
  Taught her maindenhood's disguise,
When a tenderer light came burning
  In the soft depths of her eyes.
Then she wandered down the meadows,
  Like some restless woodland elf,
Or sat hidden deep in shadows,
  Singing softly to herself,
Or repeated dreams elysian
  From some poet's touching strain,
As some vague and nameless vision
  Were half-formed within the brain.
I had counselled, led, reproved her,—
  Now the time for these was o'er;
From a baby I had loved her,
  She could be a child no more.

Then she grew a listless weeper,
  Scarce her lip might lightly speak,
And the crimson glow was deeper
  In the white snow of her cheek.
And sometimes, at midnight waking,
  I have heard her bitter sighs,
And have seen the tear-drops breaking
  Through the closed lids of her eyes.
Sometimes, like a shaken blossom,
  Moved her heart with visions sweet;
With my hand upon her bosom,
  I could feel it beat, and beat.
While her young face down the meadows
  Kept in childhood's pleasant track,
I could kiss off all the shadows,
  Other lips had kissed them back!

Oftener then the tear-dews pearly
  Dropped upon her soft white cheek,
Sorrow came to her so early,
  And her womanhood was weak.
Life grew weary, very weary:
  I had trembled, knowing well
Evermore it must be dreary,
  When the first great shadow fell.
It had fallen,—the old, sad story,
  Hope deferred, and wearying doubt;
From her youth's first crown of glory
  All the roses had dropped out.

Once, when husbandmen were bearing
  To their barns the ripened ear,
And that sorrow had been wearing
  On her mortal life a year;
As she sat with me at evening,
  Looking earnestly without,
Still half hopeful, and half yielding
  To the bitterness of doubt;
Anxiously towards me leaning,
  Breaking off a lonesome tune,
She asked, with deepest meaning,
  If the year had worn to June.
Said I, roses lately blooming
  Have all faded from their prime;
And she answered, He is coming!
  'T is the season, 't is the time!

Then she looked adown the valley
  Towards the pleasant fields in sight;

Where the wheat was hanging heavy
  And the rye was growing white;
And she said, with full heart beating
  And with earnest, trembling tone,
"If to-night should be our meeting,
  Let me see him first alone."

So with trust still unabated,
  With affection deep and true,
She watched, and hoped, and waited,
  All the lonesome summer through;
Till the autumn wind blew dreary;
  Then she almost ceased to smile,
And her spirit grew more weary
  Of its burden all the while.
I remember well of sharing
  The last watch she ever kept,
Till she turned away dispairing,
  Saying sadly while she wept:—

"Shut the window! when 't is lifted
  I can feel the cheerless rain,
And the yellow leaves are drifted
  O'er me, through the open pane.
Heavy shadows, creeping nigher,
  Darken over all the walk:
Let us sit beside the fire,
  Where we used to sit and talk.
Close the shutter, through the gloaming
  My poor eyes can see no more,
And if any one is coming
  I shall hear them at the door.

"O my friend, but speak, and cheer me,—
Speak until my heart grow light;
What if he were very near me,—
What if he should come to-night!
It might be so,—ere the morrow
He might sit there where thou art,
And the weight of all this sorrow
Be uplifted from my heart.
Idle, idle, long endurance
Changes hope to fear and doubt,
Saying oft a sweet assurance
Almost wears its meaning out.

"O, my thoughts are foolish dreaming,
Fancies of a troubled brain,
Very like the truth in seeming;
But he will not come again.
Never will his hand caress me,
Pushing back this faded hair,
Never whisper soft, 'God bless thee!'
Half in fondness, half in prayer.
Well, if he were standing near me,
Close as thou hast stood to-day,
Could I make the Father hear me,
Could I turn from him to pray?

"O my friend, whose soul was never
On such waves of passion tost,
Plead for Heaven's sweet mercy ever,
That I be not wholly lost!
Talk to me of peaceful bosoms,
Never touched by mortal ills;

Talk of beds of fragrant blossoms,
  Whitening all the fadeless hills.
Promises of sweet Evangels,
  Blessed hope of life above,
O eternity, O angels!
  Turn my thoughts from human love!"

RESOLVES.

HAVE said I would not meet him;
  Have I said the words in vain?
Sunset burns along the hill-tops,
  And I'm waiting here again.
But my promise is not broken,
  Though I stand where once we met;
When I hear his coming footsteps,
  I can fly him even yet.

We have stood here oft, when evening
  Deepened slowly o'er the plain;
But I must not, dare not, meet him
  In the shadows here again;
For I could not turn away and leave
  That pleading look and tone,
And the sorrow of his parting
  Would be bitter as my own.

In the dim and distant ether
  The first star is shining through,
And another and another
  Tremble softly in the blue:

Should I linger but one moment
  In the shadows where I stand,
I shall see the vine-leaves parted,
  With a quick, impatient hand.

But I will not wait his coming!
  He will surely come once more;
Though I said I would not meet him,
  I have told him so before;
And he knows the stars of evening
  See me standing here again,—
O, he surely will not leave me
  Now to watch and wait in vain!

'Tis the hour, the time of meeting!
  In one moment 't will be past;
And last night he stood beside me,—
  Was that blessed time the last?
I could better bear my sorrow,
  Could I live that parting o'er;
O, I wish I had not told him
  That I would not come *once* more!

Could that have been the night-wind
  Moved the branches thus apart?
Did I hear a coming footstep,
  Or the beating of my heart?
No! I hear him, I can see him,
  And my weak resolves are vain;
I will fly,—but to his bosom,
  And to leave it not again!

PROPHECIES.

AN urn within her clasped hands,
 Brimful and running o'er with
 dew
Spring on the green hills smiling
 stands,
Or walks in pleasant valley-lands,
 Through sprouting grass and violets blue.
And but this morn, almost before
 The sunshine came its leaves to gild,
In the old elm that shades our door,
 There came a timid bird to build.

O time of flowers! O time of song!
 How does my heart rejoice again!
For pleasant things to thee belong;
And desolate, and drear, and long,
 To me was Winter's lonesome reign:

Since last thou trodd'st the vale and hill,
  And nature with delight was rife,
A shadow strange, and dark, and chill,
  Has hung above my house of life.

But now I see its blackness drift
  Away, away, from out my sky;
And, as its heavy folds uplift,
There shines upon me, through the rift,
  A burning star of prophecy:
My heart is singing with the birds,
  Life's orb has passed from its eclipse;
And some sweet poet's hopeful words
  Are always, always, on my lips.

O thou who lov'st me! O my friend!
  Whate'er thy fears, where'er thou art,
As these soft skies above thee bend,
Does not their pleasant sunshine lend
  A gleam of sunshine to thy heart?
Sweet prophecies through all the day
  Within my bosom softly thrill,
And, while the night-time wears away,
  My sleep with pleasant visions fill.

And I must whisper unto thee,
  Thou, who hast waited long in vain;
Though distant still the day may be,
It shall be in our destiny
  To tread the selfsame path again;
And over hills, with blossoms white,
  Or lingering by the singing streams,
That path shall wander on in light,
  And life be happier than our dreams!

DREAMS.

HATE'ER before my sight ap-
pears,
One vision in my heart i-
borne,—
Two sweet, sad faces, wet with
tears,
Seen through the dim, gray light of morn.

And half o'ershadowing them, arise
Thoughts, which are never lulled to sleep,
Of one, whose calm, rebuking eyes
Are sadder that they do not weep.

O friend, whose lot it might not be
To tread, with me, life's path of ills!
O friend, who yet shalt walk with me
The white path of the eternal hills!

Gone are the moments when we planned
Those sweet, but unsubstantial bowers,
In some unknown and pleasant land,
Where all our future wound through flowers.

Into the past eternity
Have faded all those hopes and schemes;
That summer island in the sea
Slept only in our sea of dreams.

I know not if our hope was sin,
When that fair structure was upbuilt;
But this I know, that mine has been
The bitterest recompense of guilt.

And the wild tempest of despair
  Still sweeps my spirit like a blast;
Tears, penance, agonizing prayer,—
  Could you not save me from the past!

THE CONFESSION.

N the moonlight of the Spring-
    time,
  Trembling, blushing, half afraid,
Heard I first the fond confession
  From the sweet lips of the maid.

As the roses of the Summer,
  By his warm embraces won,
Take a fairer, richer color
  From the glances of the sun;—

So as, gazing, earnest, anxious,
  I besought her but to speak,
Deep and deeper burned the crimson
  Of the blushes in her cheek;—

Till at last, with happy impulse,
  Impulse that she might not check,
As it softly thrilled and trembled,
  Stole her white arm round my neck;—

As it softly thrilled and trembled,
Stole her white arm round my neck.

And with lips, that, half averted
From the lips that bent above,
Met the kiss of our betrothal,
Told the maiden of her love.

THE POEM.

I AM dreaming o'er a poem
  Of affection's strength sublime;
Loved, because that once I read it
  In the dear, dear olden time,
While you sat and praised my reading
  Of the poet's touching rhyme.

And how often, very gently,
  Did you check my cadence, when
I read the sweetest verses
  Over to you once again!
I have read that blessed poem
  Many, many times since then!

Then you softly closed the volume,
  When I paused at the last line,
While your eyes said sweeter poems,—
  Poems that were more divine;
And all Hybla sweets were clustered
  On the lips that dropped to mine.

This is over now, all over,—
  And 't is better thus to be;
Yet I often sit and wonder
  Who is reading soft to thee,
And if any voice is sweeter
  To thy heart than mine would be!

TO ONE WHO SANG OF LOVE.

THOU hast sung of love's confession
Out beneath the starry skies,
Of the rapture of the moment
When the soul is breathed in sighs,
And the maiden's trembling transport
As she blushingly replies
To the worship of a lover,
Breathed from speaking lips and eyes.

By the earnest tender pathos
Of thy every witching line,
Such an hour of bliss ecstatic
Has surely once been thine:
And I would that Heaven might answer
This earnest wish of mine,
That thy star of love and beauty
May wane not, nor decline.

Listening to the first confession,
Lingering o'er the first fond kiss,—
What an age of bliss is crowded
In an hour of life like this!
Surely thine at such a moment
Has been perfect happiness,
And the maiden, the fond maiden,
O, I cannot guess her bliss!

Sometimes to my heart in slumber
Thought so like the truth will steal,

That the pressure of sweet kisses
On my brow I almost feel;
And I dream fond lips have uttered
What they might no more conceal;
But I cannot, no, I cannot,
Make such blessed visions real.

ARCHIE.

TO be back in the beautiful shadow
Of that old maple-tree down in the meadow,
Watching the smiles that grew dearer and dearer,
Listening to lips that grew nearer and nearer!
O to be back in the crimson-topped clover,
Sitting again with my Archie, my lover!

O for the time when I felt his caresses
Smoothing away from my forehead the tresses,
When up from my heart to my cheek went the blushes,
As he said that my voice was as sweet as the thrush's,—
When he said that my eyes were bewitchingly jetty,
And I told him 'twas only my love made them pretty.

My Archie and I shall sit always together,
Then you may tell me of heaven for ever.

Talk not of maiden reserve and of duty,
Or hide from my vision such wonderful
beauty;

Pulses above may beat calmly and even,—
We have been fashioned for earth, and not
heaven;
Angels are perfect,—I am but a woman;
Saints may be passionless,—Archie is human.

Talk not of heavenly, down-dropping blisses,—
Can they fall on the brow like the rain of soft
kisses?
Preach not the promise of priests and evan-
gels,—
Love-crowned, I ask not the crown of the
angels;
All that the wall of pure jasper incloses
Makes not less lovely the white bridal roses.

Tell me that when all this life shall be over,
I shall still love him, and he be my lover,—
That in meadows far sweeter than clover or
heather
My Archie and I shall sit always together,
Loving eternally, wed ne'er to sever,—
Then you may tell me of heaven for ever!

MAIDEN FEARS.

HE knows that I love him;
O, how could he tell
What I thought I would keep
In my bosom so well,
By guarding each action,
Each word, I might say!

Yet he knows that I love him,—
  O, wo to the day!

To hide it I tried
  By each innocent art,
And I thought I had kept it
  Down deep in my heart:
Yet vain was my effort,
  My pride, through the past,
Since my weakness, my folly,
  Have shown it at last.

'Twas last night that he learned it,
  When down in the grove
He whispered me something
  Of hope and of love;
'Twas not that I faltered,
  I dared not to speak,—
But the blood mounted up
  From my heart to my cheek.

Not mine was the fault
  That such weakness was shown,—
O, he should not have kissed me
  By starlight alone!
And I thought, till I saw
  How he guessed at my love,
I thought that the shadows
  Were deeper above!

Nay, thou canst not console me,
  My hopes are undone;

Yet he knows that I love him,—
O, wo to the day!

He will say that too lightly
  M · heart has been won;
And this spot on my forehead
  For ever will burn,
For he knows that I love him,—
  He will not return!

He will say 'twas unmaidly
  Thus to reveal
What I might not, I could not,
  That moment conceal;
And the heart he has won
  Will cast lightly aside;—
O, I would, ere he knew it,
  I would I had died!

O thou who hast never
  Been faithless to me,
Crushed, bleeding, and broken
  My heart turns to thee:
Friend, counsellor, sister,
  Through all things the same,
Let me hide in thy bosom
  My blushes of shame!

THE UNGUARDED MOMENT.

YES, my lips to-night have spoken
  Words I said they should not speak;
And I would I could recall them,—
  Would I had not been so weak.
O that one unguarded moment!
  Were it mine to live again,
All the strength of its temptation
  Would appeal to me in vain.

True, my lips have only uttered
  What is ever in my heart:
I am happy when beside him,
  Wretched when we are apart;
Though I listen to his praises
  Always longer than I should,
Yet my heart can never hear them
  Half so often as it would!

And I would not, could not, pain him,
  Would not for the world offend,—
I would have him know I like him,
  As a brother, as a friend;
But I meant to keep one secret
  In my bosom always hid,
For I never meant to tell him
  That I loved him,—but I did.

BURNING THE LETTERS.

SAID that they were valueless,—
  I 'd rather have them not,—
All that since made them precious
  Was, or should have been, forgot;
I would do it very willingly,
  And not because I ought,—
But I did not, somehow, find it
  Quite so easy as I thought.

One was full of pleasant flattery;—
  I do not think I 'm vain,
And yet I paused a moment
  To read it once again.
One repeated dear, old phrases
  I had heard a thousand times;
I had read him once some verses,
  And another praised my rhymes.

One was just exactly like him,—
  Such a pretty little note!
One was interspersed with poetry
  That lovers always quote.
I don't know why I read them
  Unless 't was just to know,
Since they once had been so precious,
  What had ever made them so.

I had told him when we parted
  To think no more of me;
And I 'm sure he 's nothing to me,—
  Indeed, why should he be?
Yet the flame sunk down to ashes,
  And I sat and held them still;
But I said that I would burn them,—
  And, some other time, I will!

NELLY.

I'M glad you "don't love him,"
I really did fear
(Nay, frown not so terribly,
Nelly, my dear;)
His voice was so witching,
His eyes were so bright,
Though you did not yet love him,
I feared that you might!

So you're candid, now, Nelly,
You're telling me true,
"His voice never sounded
Bewitching to you."
Yet I sometimes have thought,
When you heard his soft tone,
That a little more tenderness
Spoke in your own.

And you're sure you don't care, now,
  My dear little elf,
" Who else he talks love to,

Though you did not yet love him,
I feared that you might!

  So 't is not yourself."
Sometimes when your forehead
  Such crimson would take,

I suspected—no matter,
  I've made a mistake.

Nay, do not now, Nelly,
  O, do not be mad!
Since you say you don't love him,
  It makes me so glad;
Because I would never
  Have told it, you see,
But honestly, darling,
  He's talked love to me!

Are you glad he has done
  What you wished him to do,—
That he talked about love
  To another than you?
Yes, you surely must feel
  Quite a sense of relief;—
But those tears are not joyous,
  That sob is like grief!

He said he had hidden it
  Long in his breast;—
How you tremble!—nay, listen,
  I'll tell you the rest.
He said, just as true
  As I sit here alive,
That he loved you, dear Nelly,—
  Aha! you revive!

A LAMENT.

ONCE in the season of childhood's joy,
Dreaming never of life's great ills,
Hand in hand with a happy boy,
I walked about on my native hills,—

Gathering berries ripe and fair,
Pressing them oft to his smiling lip,
Braiding flowers in his sunny hair,
And letting the curls through my fingers slip,—

Watching the clouds of the evening pass
Over the moon in her home of blue;
Or chasing fireflies over the grass,
Till our feet were wet with the summer dew.

Now I walk on the hills alone,
Dreaming never of hope or joy,
And over a dungeon's floor of stone
Sweep the curls of that happy boy.

And every night when a rose-hedge springs
Up from the ashes of sunset's pyre,
And the eve-star, folding her golden wings,
Drops like a bird in the leaves of fire,—

I sit and think how he entered in,
And farther and farther, every time,

Followed the downward way of sin,
  Till it led to the awful gates of crime.

I sit and think, till my great despair
  Rises up like a mighty wave,
How fast the locks of my father's hair
  Are whitening now for the quiet grave.

I walked about on my native hills,—
Gathering berries ripe and fair.

But never reproach on my lip has been,
  Never one moment can I forget,
Though bound in prison and lost in sin,
  My brother once is my brother yet.

THE LULLABY.

THROUGH the open summer lattice,
Half revealed and half in shade,
Yesternight I saw a mortal
Whose remembrance will not fade.

Little birds their heads had hidden
Under wings of gold and brown;
Lily bells and luscious blossoms
Softly had been folded down;

Fountains with their quiet dropping,
Only lulled the drowsy bees;
And the wind was lightly going
In and out the tops of trees;

But the pale and restless creature—
Had she dreamed too much before?—
Seemed as one whom sleep would visit
Never, never, never more.

Rocking by the summer lattice,
Rocking to and fro, she sung,

O, the saddest, saddest music
  Ever fell from mortal tongue!

So she strove to hush the crying,
  Bitterer that 't was faint and low,
Of the little baby pressing
  Close against her heart of wo.

And her words were very mournful,
  And so very, very faint;
She was keeping down her anguish,
  That no ear might hear her plaint.

"Lullaby, my wretched baby;
  Go to sleep, and sleep till morn!
Lullaby, my wretched baby;
  Would that thou hadst not been born!

"Mock me not with open eyelids,
  For thine eyes are soft and blue;
While in mine the midnight blackness
  Deepens, looking down on you.

"Time shall bind about your forehead
  Sunny hair in golden bands;
Tangle not my raven tresses
  With your soft and clinging hands!

"Lullaby, my wretched baby;
  O, how long the watches seem!
Lullaby, my wretched baby;
  Dream and smile, and smile and dream!

"O the sad eyes of my mother!
  O my brother, proud and brave!
O the white hair of my father,
  Drooping sadly toward the grave!

"O my sister, pure as heaven,
  Here thy head in sleep has lain!
Never on this wretched bosom
  Canst thou pillow it again!

"Lullaby, my wretched baby;
  Live I only for thy sake!
Lullaby, my wretched baby;
  Sleep, and dream, and never wake!"

LEFT ALONE.

SHE'S left me here alone again:
  'T will be a weary lot,
Through all this cheerless winter time
  To live where she is not;
To sit, where once we used to sit,
  With smileless lip and dumb;
To count the moments since she went,
  And know not when she'll come!

We talked through all the summer time,
  We'd talked through all the spring,
Of how upon the winter hearth
  We'd make a pleasant ring;

Of how with loving words and looks
  The time should all be sped;—
The firelight's glow is mournful now,
  The books are all unread.

We never were together long,
  We have not been so blest;
I might have known this hope of ours
  Would perish like the rest:
And half I trembled all the while,
  And feared it would be so;—
The hand of fate would press me back
  From where her feet must go.

If there shall ever be a time,
  When, as in days that were,
My soul can whisper all its dreams
  And all its thoughts to her,—
When I can share her heart's sweet hopes,
  Or soothe its bitter pain,—
I would the hours were past till then,
  And that were come again!

THE RETROSPECT.

AS one who sees life's hopes have end,
  And cannot hush the bitter cry,
Thou weep'st for that lost vale, my friend,
  Where childhood's pleasant places lie;
And looking down the sloping track
  Where now our lonesome steps are told,

Wouldst softly roll the seasons back,
And leave us children as of old.

**Wouldst softly roll the seasons back,
And leave us children as of old.**

Nay, weave sweet fancies as you will,
Yet what is childish happiness

To such great rapture as can fill
The heart of womanhood with bliss?
And though the trials which years must bring
Have come, and left thee what thou art,
Think what a great and wondrous thing
Is victory o'er the human heart!

Life's sparkling wine for us is dim,
Only the bitter drops remain;
Yet for the brightness on the brim,
Who would not drink the draught of pain?
And not in even ways, my friend,
Attains the soul to regions higher;
If step by step our feet ascend,
Their path must be a path of fire!

ONE SHALL BE TAKEN.

EAR friend, whose presence always made
Even the dreariest night-time glad,—
Whose lengthening absence darkens o'er
The little sunshine that I had,—
My heart is sad for thee to-night,
And every wretched thought of mine
Reaches across the lonesome hills,
That lie between my home and thine.

O woods, wherein our childish feet,
  Gathering the summer blossoms, strayed!
O meadows, white with clover-blooms!
  O soft, green hollows, where we played!
Can you not cool that aching brow,
  With all your shadows and your dew;
And charm the slow and languid step
  Back to the joyous life it knew?

Most loved, most cherished, since that hour
  When, as she blest thee o'er and o'er,
Our mother put thee from her arms,
  To feel thy kisses never more;
And I, that scarce were missed, am spared,
  While o'er thy way the shadow lies,—
Infinite Mercy surely knew
  Thou wert the fittest for the skies!

THE BROTHERS.

WE had no home, we only had
  A shelter for our head:
How poor we were, how scantily
  We all were clothed and fed!
But though a wretched little child,
  I know not why or how,
I did not feel it half so much
  As I can feel it now!

When mother sat at night and sewed,
  My rest was calm and deep;

She wrapped the covering round our bed,
In many an ample fold.

I did not know that she was tired,
Or that she needed sleep.
She wrapped the covering round our bed,
In many an ample fold;
She had not half so much herself
To keep her from the cold.

I know it now, I know it all,—
 They knew it then above,—
Her life of patient sacrifice,
 And never-tiring love.
I know, for then her tasks seemed done,—
 We all were grown beside,—
How glad she must have been to go,
 After the baby died!

I do not care to deck me now
 With costly robe or gaud,—
My mother dressed so plain at home,
 And never went abroad.
I do not even want a shroud
 Of linen, white and pure,—
They made our little baby one
 That was so coarse and poor.

I had another brother then,
 I prayed that God would save;
I knew not life had darker dooms
 Than lying in the grave.
I did not know, when o'er the dead
 So bitterly I cried,
I'd live to wish a thousand times
 The other, too, had died.

REMORSE.

SWEETEST friend I ever had,
How sinks my heavy heart to know
That life, which was so bright for thee,
Has lost its sunshine and its glow!

I cannot think of thee as one
Sighing for calm repose in vain;
Nor of the beauty of thy smile,
Faded and sadly dim with pain.

Thou surely shouldst not be to-day
Lying upon the autumn leaves,
But in the borderfields of hope,
Binding the blossoms into sheaves.

For, with a shadow on thy way,
The sunshine of my life is o'er,
And flowery dell and fresh green holt
Can charm my footsteps nevermore!

And if I have not always seen
The beauty of thy deeds aright,—
If I have failed to make thy path
As smooth and even as I might,—

Not thine the fault, but mine the sin,
And I have felt its heaviest curse
Fall on the heart that aches to-day,
With vain repentance and remorse,—

A heart that lifts its cry to thee,
  Above this wild and awful blast,
That sweeping from the hills of home,
  Brings bitterest memories of the past.

O, sweet forgiveness, from thy love,
  Send to me o'er the waste between;
Not as thou hop'st to be forgiven,
  For thou hast never bowed to sin.

Pure as thy light of life was given,
  Thou still hast kept its steady flame;
And the chaste garment of thy soul
  Is white and spotless as it came.

PROPHECY.

NO great sea lifts its angry waves
  Between me and the friend most dear,
And over all our household graves
  The grass has grown for many a year.

With all that makes the heart rejoice,
  The days of summer go and come;
No feeble step, no failing voice,
  Saddens the chambers of our home.

Yet, though I know, and feel, and see,
  God's blessings all about my way,
The burden of sad prophecy
  Lies heavy on my soul to-day.

These awful words of destiny
  Are sounding in my heart and brain:
"Not an unbroken family
  Shall summer find us here again!"

O God! if this indeed be so,
  Whose pillow then shall be unprest?
Whose heart, that feels life's pleasant glow,
  Shall faint, and beat itself to rest?

Eternal silence makes reply,
  We may not, cannot, know our doom;
No voice comes downward from the sky,
  No voice comes upward from the tomb.

Yet this I would not ask in vain:
  Hide from my wretched eyes the day
When by our household graves again
  The turf is lightly put away!

First from our home, though all descend
  At last to that one place of rest,
O solemn Earth! O mighty Friend!
  Take me and hide me in thy breast!

THE CONSECRATION.

O SOUL, that must survive that hour
  When heart shall fail and flesh decay!
God, angels, men, are witnesses
  Of vows which thou hast made to-day.

What solemn fears this hour are born,
  What joyful hopes this hour are given!
Thought reaches down from heaven to hell,
  And up from farthest hell to heaven.

Before my fearful vision pass
  Those star-like souls, grown darkly dim,—
The sea of mingled glass and fire,
  The saints and priests with conquering hymn.
O God! shall I go down with those,
  Wandering through blackness from their place,
Or up with the redeemed and saved,
  Who stand before their Father's face?

For now my eyes have seen the truth,
  This is thy sure and just decree:
"If I shall turn again to sin,
  There is no sacrifice for me;"
And the baptismal touch, which lay
  So lightly on the brow beneath,
Shall be omnipotent in power,
  To press me surely down to death.

Its seal shall be a diadem,
  To shine amid the angel choir,
Or on my forehead burn in hell,
  An everlasting crown of fire;
And all who hear my vows to-day
  Shall hear my final sentence read:
God, angels, men, are witnesses
  At the great judgment of the dead.

DRAWING WATER.

I HAD drunk, with lip unsated,
Where the founts of pleasure burst;
I had hewn out broken cisterns,
And they mocked my spirit's thirst:

And I said, life is a desert,
Hot, and measureless, and dry;
And God will not give me water,
Though I pray, and faint, and die.

Spoke there then a friend and brother,
"Rise, and roll the stone away;
There are founts of life upspringing
In thy pathway every day."

Then I said my heart was sinful,
Very sinful was my speech;
All the wells of God's salvation
Are too deep for me to reach.

And he answered, "Rise and labor,-
Doubt and idleness is death;
Shape thee out a goodly vessel
With the strong hands of thy faith."

So I wrought and shaped the vessel,
  Then knelt lowly, humbly there,
And I drew up living water
  With the golden chain of prayer.

THE DREAMER.

BLOW life's most fearful tempest blow,
  And make the midnight wild and rough;
My soul shall battle with you now,—
  I've been a dreamer long enough!

Open, O sea, a darker path,
  Dash to my lips the angry spray;
The tenth wave of thy fiercest wrath
  Were nothing to my strength to-day!

Though floating onward listlessly
  When pleasant breezes softly blew,
My spirit with the adverse sea
  Shall rise, and gather strength anew.

Wake, soul of mine, and be thou strong;
  Keep down thy weakness, human heart;
Thou hast unnerved my arm too long,
  O foolish dreamer that thou art!

For I have sat and mused for hours
  Of havens that I yet should see,
Of winding paths, of pleasant flowers,
  And summer islands in the sea,—

Forgetful of the storms that come,
  Of winds that dig the ocean grave,
And sharp reefs hidden by the foam
  That drifts like blossoms on the wave,—

Forgetful, too, that he who guides
  Must have a firm and steadfast hand,
If e'er his vessel safely rides
  Through storm and breaker to the land,—

Idly and listless drifting on,
  Feeding my fancy all the while,
As lovesick dreamers feed upon
  The honeyed sweetness of a smile.

Fool that I was,—ay! Folly's mock,—
  To think not, in those pleasant hours,
How barks have foundered on the rock,
  And drifted past the isles of flowers!

Yet well it were, if, roused to feel,
  I yet avert such fearful fate,—
The quick, sharp grating of the keel
  Had been a warning all too late.

But courage still; for whether now
  Or rough or smooth life's ocean seems,
To-day my soul records her vow,
  Hereafter I am done with dreams!

SOLEMNITY OF LIFE.

HETHER are cast our destinies
In peaceful ways, or ways of strife;
A solemn thing to us it is,
This mystery of human life.

Solemn, when first, unconscious, dumb,
Within an untried world we stand,
Immortal beings that have come
Newly from God's creating hand.

And solemn, even as 'tis fleet,
The time when, learning childish fears,
We cross, with scarcely balanced feet,
The threshold of our mortal years.

'Tis solemn, when, with parting smiles,
We leave its innocence and truth,
To learn how deeper than the child's
Are all the loves and fears of youth.

It is a solemn thing to snap
The cords of human love apart;
More solemn still to feel them wrap
Their wondrous strength about the heart.

'Tis solemn to have ever known
The pleadings of the soul unmoved,—
Solemn to feel ourselves alone;
More solemn still to be beloved.

It is a solemn thing to wear
The roses of the bridal wreath,—
Solemn the words we utter there,
Of faith unchanging until death.

Solemn is life, when God unlocks
The fountain in the soul most deep,—
Solemn the heart-beat, when it rocks
A young immortal to its sleep.

'Tis solemn when the Power above
Darkens our being's living spark,—
Solemn to see the friends we love
Going downward from us to the dark.

O human life, when all thy woes
And all thy trials are struggled through,
What can eternity disclose
More wondrous solemn than we knew!

MY BLESSINGS.

GREAT waves of plenty rolling up
Their golden billows to our feet,
Fields where the ungathered rye is white,
Or heavy with the yellow wheat;

Wealth surging inward from the sea,
And plenty through our land abroad,
With sunshine resting over all,
That everlasting smile of God!

For these, yet not for these alone,
  My tongue its gratitude would say:
All the great blessings of my life
  Are present in my thought to-day.

For more than all my mortal wants
  Have been, O God, thy full supplies;—
Health, shelter, and my daily bread,
  For these my grateful thanks arise.

For ties of faith, whose wondrous strength
  Time nor eternity can part;
For all the words of love that fall
  Like living waters on my heart;

For even that fearful strife, where sin
  Was conquered and subdued at length,
Temptations met and overcome,
  Whereby my soul has gathered strength;

For all the warnings that have come
  From mortal agony of death;
For even that bitterest storm of life,
  Which drove me on the rock of faith.

For all the past I thank thee, God!
  And for the future trust in thee,
Whate'er of trial or blessing yet,
  Asked or unasked, thou hast for me.

Yet only this one boon I crave,—
  After life's brief and fleeting hour,
Make my beloved thy beloved,
  And keep us in thy day of power!

SABBATH THOUGHTS.

I AM sitting all the while
Looking down the solemn aisle,
Toward the saints and martyrs old,
Standing in their niches cold,—
Toward the wing of cherubs fair,
Veiling half their golden hair,
And the painted light that falls
Through the window on the walls.

I can see the revered flow
Of soft garments, white as snow,
And the shade of silver hair
Dropping on the book of prayer.
I can hear the litany,
"Miserable sinners, we!"
And the organ swelling higher,
And the chanting of the choir.

And I marvel if with them,
In the New Jerusalem,
I shall hear the sacred choir
Chant with flaming tongues of fire;
If I e'er shall find a place
With the ransomed, saved by grace;
If my feet shall ever tread
Where the just are perfected?

Not, my soul, as now thou art;
Not with this rebellious heart;
Not with nature unsubdued,
Evil overshadowing good;

Not while I for pardon seek
With a faith so faint and weak;
Not while tempted thus to sin,
From without and from within'

Thou whom love did once compel
Down from heaven to sleep in hell;
Thou whose mercy purged from dross
Even the thief upon the cross,
Save me, O thou bleeding Lamb,
Chief of sinners though I am,
When, with clouds about thee furled,
Thou shalt come to judge the world!

NEARER HOME.

NE sweetly solemn thought
  Comes to me o'er and o'er,—
I am nearer home to-day
  Than I have ever been be-
    fore;—

Nearer my Father's house
  Where the many mansions be;
Nearer the great white throne,
  Nearer the jasper sea;—

Nearer the bound of life
  Where we lay our burdens down;
Nearer leaving the cross,
  Nearer gaining the crown

But lying darkly between,
  Winding down through the night,
Is the dim and unknown stream
  That leads at last to the light.

Closer and closer my steps
  Come to the dark abysm;
Closer death to my lips
  Presses the awful chrysm.

Father, perfect my trust;
  Strengthen the might of my faith;
Let me feel as I would when I stand
  On the rock of the shore of death,—

Feel as I would when my feet
  Are slipping o'er the brink;
For it may be I 'm nearer home,—
  Nearer now than I think.

HYMN.

OD of the Sabbath, calm and still,
  Father, in whom we live and move,
How do our trembling bosoms thrill
  With words which tell us of thy love!

Thine heralds, speaking of the tomb,
  The organ's voice, the censer's flame,
The solemn minister's shadowy gloom,
  Awe us, and make us fear thy name.

The earthquake, opening deep its graves,
  The lightning, running down the sky,
The great sea, lifting up its waves.
  Speak of thine awful majesty!

But once thou camest in Eden's prime,
  Lord of the soul, to talk with men,
And in the cool of eventime
  Thou seemest with us, now as then.

For when our trembling souls draw near,
  And silence keeps the earth and sea,
Thou speak'st, with no interpreter
  To stand between our hearts and thee!

SOWING SEED.

O and sow beside all waters,
  In the morning of thy youth,
In the evening scatter broadcast
  Precious seeds of living truth.

For though much may sink and perish
  In the rocky, barren mould,
And the harvest of thy labor
  May be less than thirty-fold,

Let thy hand be not withholden,
  Still beside all waters sow,
For thou know'st not which shall prosper,
  Whether this or that will grow,

While some precious portion, scattered,
  Germinating, taking root,
Shall spring up, and grow, and ripen
  Into never-dying fruit.

Therefore, sow beside all waters,
  Trusting, hoping, toiling on;
When the fields are white for harvest,
  God will send his angels down.

And thy soul may see the value
  Of its patient morns and eves,
When the everlasting garner
  Shall be filled with precious sheaves.

THE BAPTISM.

FROM the waters of affliction,
  From her baptism of dark wo,
With her sweet eyes very mournful,
  And her forehead like the snow,

Came she up; and, O, how many
  In such hours of trial are seen,
When they faint with mortal weakness,
  Knowing not whereon to lean!

With her face upon my bosom,
  Said she then in accent sad,
As she wound her arms about me,
  I was all the friend she had.

And I told her—pushing backward
  From her forehead like the snow,
All her tear-wet tresses, dripping
  With that baptism of dark wo—

How, in all that great affliction,
  Loving hands had led her on,
When she came up from the waters,
  Led her when her feet went down,—

And that only the good Father,
  He who thus her faith had tried,
Could have brought her through the billows
  Safely to the other side.

And I told her how life's pilgrim
  Crossed that solemn stream beneath.
To a brighter pathway leading,
  Up the living hills of faith.

Lifting upward from my bosom
  Then her forehead like the snow,
I will weep, she said, no longer,
  Therefore rise and let us go!

And, as one who walks untroubled
  By no mortal doubt or fear,
Oft we heard her far above us,
  Singing hymns of lofty cheer,—

Till with feet that firmly balanced
  On faith's summit-rock she trod,
And beheld the shining bastions
  Of the city of our God.

Then her voice was tenderer, holier,
  She grew gentler all the while;
It was like a benediction
  But to see her patient smile.

As she walked with cheerful spirit
  Where her daily duties led,
"Father, keep me from temptation,"
  Was the only prayer she said.

Often made she earnest pleading,
  As she went from us apart,
To be saved through all her lifetime
  From the weakness of her heart.

And she prayed that she might never,
  Never in her trials below,
Bring her soul before the altar,
  Wailing in unchastened wo.

So her hands of faith were strengthened,
  And when clouds about her lay,
From her bosom all the darkness
  She could softly put away.

Smilingly she went unaided,
  When we would have led her on,
Saying always to our pleading,
  Better that I go alone.

Turned she from the faces dearest
  When her feet more feebly trod,

That she might not then be tempted
 By a mortal love from God.

So the Father, for her pleading,
 Kept her safe through all life's hours,
And her path went brightly upward
 To eternity through flowers.

THE CHRISTIAN WOMAN.

BEAUTIFUL as Morning in those hours
 When, as her pathway lies along the hills,
Her golden fingers wake the dewy flowers,
 And softly touch the waters of the rills,
Was she who walked more faintly day by day,
Till silently she perished by the way.

It was not hers to know that perfect heaven
 Of passionate love returned by love as deep,
Not hers to sing the cradle-song at even,
 Watching the beauty of her babe asleep;
"Mother and brethren,"—these she had not known,
Save such as do the Father's will alone.

Yet found she something still for which to live,—

Hearths desolate, where angel-like she came;
And "little ones," to whom her hand could give
A cup of water in her Master's name;
And breaking hearts, to bind away from death
With the soft hand of pitying love and faith.

She never won the voice of popular praise,
But counting earthly triumph as but dross,
Seeking to keep her Saviour's perfect ways,
Bearing in quiet paths his blessed cross,
She made her life, while with us here she trod,
A consecration to the will of God.

And she hath lived and labored not in vain:
Through the deep prison-cells her accents thrill,
And the sad slave leans idly on his chain,
And hears the music of her singing still;
While little children, with their innocent praise,
Keep freshly in men's hearts her Christian ways.

And what a beautiful lesson she made known?
The whiteness of her soul sin could not dim;
Ready to lay down on God's altar-stone
The dearest treasure of her life for him,
Her flame of sacrifice never, never waned;
How could she live and die so self-sustained?

For friends supported not her parting soul,
And whispered words of comfort, kind and sweet,
When treading onward to that final goal,
Where the still Bridegroom waited for her feet;
Alone she walked, yet with a fearless tread,
Down to Death's chamber and his bridal bed!

THE HOSTS OF THOUGHT.

OW heavy fall the evening shades,
Making the earth more dark and drear,
As to its sunset sadly fades
This, the last Sabbath of the year!

Oft, when the light has softly burned
Among the clouds, as day was done,
I've watched their golden furrows turned
By the red ploughshare of the sun.

To-night, no track of billowy gold
Is softly slanting down the skies;
But dull-gray bastions, dark and cold,
Shut all the glory from my eyes.

And in the plain that lies below,
What cheerless prospect meets my eye!
One long and level reach of snow,
Stretching to meet the western sky!

While far across these lonesome vales,
  Like a lost soul, and unconfined,
Down through the mountain gorges wails
  The awful spirit of the wind.

When, yester-eve, the twilight stilled,
  With soft, caressing hand, the day,
Upon my heart, that joyous thrilled,
  A sweet, tumultuous vision lay.

To-night, in sorrow's arms enwound,
  I think of broken faith and trust,
And tresses, from their flowers unbound,
  Hid in the dimness of the dust.

And hopes that took their heavenward flight,
  As fancy lately gave them birth,
Slow through the solemn air to-night
  Are beating backward to the earth.

O memory, if the shadowy hand
  Lock all thy death-crypts close and fast,
Call not my spirit back to stand
  In the dark chamber of the past!

For trembling fear, and mortal doubt,
  About me all day long have been;
So even the dreary world without
  Is brighter than the world within.

Pale hosts of thought before me start:
O for that needed power I lack,
To guard the fortress of my heart,
And press their awful columns back!

O for a soul to meet their gaze,
And grapple fearless with its wo!
As the wild *athlete*, of old days,
In the embraces of the foe!

Thoughts of the many lost and loved,—
Each unfulfilled and noble plan,—
Memories of Sabbaths unimproved,—
Duty undone to God or man;—

They come, with solemn, warning frown,
Like ghosts about some haunted tent;
And courage silently goes down,
Before their dreadful armament.

O friend of mine, in years agone,
Where'er, at this dark hour, thou art,
Why hast thou left me here alone,
To fight the battles of the heart?

Alone? A soft eye's tender light
Is turned to meet my anxious glance;
And, struggling upward from the night,
My soul has broken from her trance.

Love is omnipotent to check
  Such 'wildering fancies of the brain;
A soft hand trembles on my neck,
  And lo, I sit with hope again!

Even the sky no longer seems
  Like a dull barrier, built afar;
And through its crumbling wall there gleams
  The sweet flame of one burning star.

The winds, that from the mountain's brow
  Came down the dreary plains to sweep,
Back, in the cavernous hollow, now
  Have softly sung themselves to sleep.

Come, thou, whose love no waning knows,
  And put thy gentle hand in mine,
For strong in faith my spirit grows,
  Leaning confidingly on thine.

And in the calm, or in the strife,
  If side by side with thee I move,
Hereafter I will live a life
  That shall not shame thy trusting love.

Memory and fear, with all their powers,
  No more my soul shall crush or bend;
For the great future still is ours,
  And thou art with me, O my friend!

OUR HOMESTEAD.

OUR old brown homestead reared its walls,
From the way-side dust aloof,
Where the apple-boughs could almost cast
Their fruitage on its roof:
And the cherry-tree so near it grew,
That when awake I've lain,
In the lonesome nights, I've heard the limbs,
As they creaked against the pane:
And those orchard trees, O those orchard trees!
I've seen my little brothers rocked
In their tops by the summer breeze.

The sweet-brier under the window-sill,
  Which the early birds made glad,
And the damask rose by the garden fence,
  Were all the flowers we had.
I've looked at many a flower since then,
  Exotics rich and rare,
That to other eyes were lovelier,
  But not to me so fair;
O those roses bright, O those roses bright!
  I have twined them with my sister's locks,
That are hid in the dust from sight!

We had a well, a deep old well,
  Where the spring was never dry,
And the cool drops down from the mossy stones
  Were falling constantly:
And there never was water half so sweet
  As that in my little cup,
Drawn up to the curb by the rude old sweep,
  Which my father's hand set up;
And that deep old well, O that deep old well!
  I remember yet the splashing sound
Of the bucket as it fell.

Our homestead had an ample hearth,
  Where at night we loved to meet;
There my mother's voice was always kind,
  And her smile was always sweet;
And there I've sat on my father's knee,
  And watched his thoughtful brow,
With my childish hand in his raven hair,—
  That hair is silver now!

But that broad hearth's light, O that broad
hearth's light!
And my father's look, and my mother's
smile,—
They are in my heart to-night.

THE BOOK OF POEMS.

N the pages whose rhymed music
So oft has chimed thine ears,
I have gazed till my heart is filling
With memories of vanished
years;
And, leaving the lines of the poet,
Has sadly turned to roam
Away to that beautiful valley
In the sunset land of home!

O land of the greenest pastures,
O land of the coolest streams.
Shall I only again be near you
In the shadowy light of dreams?
Shall I only sit in visions
By the hearth and the lattice-pane,
And my friend of the past, my brother,
Shall we meet not there again?

As a sweet memorial ever
This book to my heart will be;
But I never can read its pages
So far from home and thee;
For the words grow dim before me,
Or tremble on my lips,
And the disc of life's orb of beauty,
Is darkened with wo's eclipse.

So for ever closed and clasped
  Shall the volume lie unread,
As might in some ancient cloister
  The gift of the saintly dead,
Till our hands shall open its pages
  Once more beneath that dome
That hangs over the beautiful valley,
  In the sunset land of home!

TO FRANK.

'IS three years and something over
  Since I looked upon you last,
But I only think about you
  As I saw you in the past.

And when memory recalls you,
  As she has done to-day,
You're just as young, and just as small,
  As when you went away.

I can see you hunt for flowers
  In the meadows green and sweet,
Or go wading through the hollows
  With your little, naked feet;—

Or peeping through the bushes
  That hedged the garden round,
To see if any little birds
  Were in the nest you'd found.

And I know how in the clover,
  Where the bees were used to come,
You held them down beneath your hat,
  To hear their pleasant hum.

And how in summer evenings,
  Through the door-yard wet with dew,
The watch-dog led you many a chase,—
  He's growing older too!

I know when on the dear old porch
  We coaxed you first to walk,
And treasured every word you said
  When you began to talk.

We asked you what you meant to be,
  And laughed at your replies,
Because you said, when you grew up
  To manhood, you'd be wise.

And may you pray the God of love,
  And I will pray him too,
To make you wise in every thing
  That makes man good and true!

MORNING.

ADLY, when the day was done,
To his setting waned the sun;
Heavily the shadows fell,
And the wind with fitful swell,
Echoed through the forest dim
Like a friar's ghostly hymn.

Mournful on the wall, afar,
Walked the evening sentry-star;
Burning clear, and cold, and lone,
Midnight's constellations shone;
While the hours, with solemn tread,
Passed like watchers by the dead.

Now at last the Morning wakes,
And the spell of darkness breaks,
On the mountains, dewy sweet,
Standing with her rosy feet,
While her golden fingers fair
Part the soft flow of her hair.

With the dew from flower and leaf
Flies the heavy dew of grief;
From the darkness of my thought,
Night her solemn aspect caught;
And the morning's joys begin,
As a morning breaks within.

God's free sunshine on the hills,
Soft mists hanging o'er the rills,
Blushing flowers of loveliness
Trembling with the light wind's kiss,—
O, the soul forgets its care,
Looking on a world so fair!

Morning wooes me with her charms,
Like a lover's pleading arms;
Soft above me bend her skies,
As a lover's tender eyes;
And my heavy heart of pain,
Trembling, thrills with hope again.

DAWN.

HE sunken moon was down an hour agone;—
And now the little silver cloud, that leant
So lovingly above her as she went,

Is changing with the touches of the dawn:
For from the clasped arms of the sweet night,
Lo! the young Dawn has gently stolen away,
And stars, that late burned with an intense ray,
Fade to a wannish, melancholy light.
A moment, smiling on the hills she stands,
Parting the curtains of the East away;
Then lightly, with her white caressing hands,
Touches the trembling eyelids of the Day;
And, leaning o'er his couch of rosy beams,
Wooes him with kisses softly from his dreams.

PARODIES.

MARTHA HOPKINS.

A BALLAD OF INDIANA.

FROM the kitchen, Martha Hopkins, as she stands there making pies,
Southward looks, along the turnpike, with her hand above her eyes;
Where, along the distant hill-side, her yearling heifer feeds,
And a little grass is growing in a mighty sight of weeds.

All the air is full of noises, for there isn't any
school,
And boys, with turned-up pantaloons, are
wading in the pool;
Blithely frisk unnumbered chickens, cackling,
for they cannot laugh;
Where the airy summits brighten, nimbly
leaps the little calf.

Gentle eyes of Martha Hopkins! tell me
wherefore do ye gaze
On the ground that's being furrowed for the
planting of the maize?
Tell me wherefore down the valley ye have
traced the turnpike's way,
Far beyond the cattle-pasture, and the brick-
yard, with its clay?

Ah! the dog-wood tree may blossom, and the
door-yard grass may shine,
With the tears of amber dropping from the
washing on the line,
And the morning's breath of balsam lightly
brush her freckled cheek,—
Little recketh Martha Hopkins of the tales of
spring they speak.

When the summer's burning solstice on the
scanty harvest glowed,
She had watched a man on horseback riding
down the turnpike-road;
Many times she saw him turning, looking
backward quite forlorn,
Till amid her tears she lost him, in the shadow
of the barn.

Ere the supper-time was over, he had passed
the kiln of brick,
Crossed the rushing Yellow River, and had
forded quite a creek,
And his flatboat load was taken, at the time
for pork and beans,
With the traders of the Wabash, to the wharf
at New Orleans.

Therefore watches Martha Hopkins holding
in her hand the pans,
When the sound of distant footsteps seems
exactly like a man's;
Not a wind the stove-pipe rattles, nor a door
behind her jars,
But she seems to hear the rattle of his letting
down the bars.

Often sees she men on horseback, coming
down the turnpike rough,
But they come not as John Jackson, she can
see it well enough;
Well she knows the sober trotting of the
sorrel horse he keeps,
As he jogs along at leisure, with his head
down like a sheep's.

She would know him 'mid a thousand, by his
home-made coat and vest;
By his socks, which were blue woollen, such
as farmers wear out west;
By the color of his trousers, and his saddle,
which was spread
By a blanket which was taken for that pur-
pose from the bed.

None like he the yoke of hickory on the
unbroken ox can throw,
None amid his father's cornfields use like him
the spade and hoe;
And at all the apple-cuttings, few indeed the
men are seen,
That can dance with him the Polka, touch
with him the violin.

He has said to Martha Hopkins, and she
thinks she hears him now,
For she knows as well as can be, that he
meant to keep his vow,
When the buckeye tree has blossomed, and
your uncle plants his corn,
Shall the bells of Indiana usher in the wed-
ding morn.

He has pictured his relations, each in Sunday
hat and gown,
And he thinks he 'll get a carriage, and they
'll spend a day in town;
That their love will newly kindle, and what
comfort it will give,
To sit down to the first breakfast, in the
cabin where they 'll live.

Tender eyes of Martha Hopkins! what has
got you in such scrape?
'T is a tear that falls to glitter on the ruffle of
her cape.
Ah! the eyes of love may brighten, to be
certain what it sees,
One man looks much like another, when half
hidden by the trees.

But her eager eyes rekindle, she forgets the pies and bread,
As she sees a man on horseback, round the corner of the shed.
Now tie on another apron, get the comb and smooth your hair,
'T is the sorrel horse that gallops, 't is John Jackson's self that's there!

WORSER MOMENTS.

HAT fellow's voice! how often steals
Its cadence o'er my lonely days!
Like something sent on wagon-wheels,
Or packed in an unconscious chaise.
I might forget the words he said
When all the children fret and cry,
But when I get them off to bed,
His gentle tone comes stealing by,
And years of matrimony flee,
And leave me sitting on his knee.

The times he came to court a spell,
The tender things he said to me,
Make me remember mighty well
My hopes that he'd propose to me.
My face is uglier, and perhaps
Time and the comb have thinned my hair,
And plain and common are the caps
And dresses that I have to wear;
But memory is ever yet
With all that fellow's flatteries writ.

Worser Moments.

I have been out at milking-time
  Beneath a dull and rainy sky,
When in the barn 'twas time to feed,
  And calves were bawling lustily,—
When scattered hay, and sheaves of oats,
  And yellow corn-ears, sound and hard,
And all that makes the cattle pass
  With wilder fleetness through the yard,—
When all was hateful, then have I,
  With friends who had to help me milk,
Talked of his wife most spitefully,
  And how he kept her dressed in silk;
And when the cattle, running there,
  Threw over me a shower of mud,
That fellow's voice came on the air,
  Like the light chewing of the cud
And resting near some speckled cow
  The spirit of a woman's spite,
I've poured a low and fervent vow
  To make him, if I had the might,
Live all his lifetime just as hard,
And milk his cows in such a yard.

I have been out to pick up wood,
  When night was stealing from the dawn,
Before the fire was burning good,
  Or I had put the kettle on
The little stove,—when babes were waking
  With a low murmur in the beds,
And melody by fits was breaking
  Above their little yellow heads,—
And this when I was up perhaps
From a few short and troubled naps,—
  And when the sun sprang scorchingly
And freely up, and made us stifle,

And fell upon each hill and tree
The bullets from his subtle rifle,—
I say a voice has thrilled me then,
Hard by that solemn pile of wood,
Or creeping from the silent glen,
Like something on the unfledged brood,
Hath stricken me, and I have pressed
Close in my arms my load of chips,
And pouring forth the hatefulest
Of words that ever passed my lips,
Have felt my woman's spirit rush
On me, as on that milking night,
And, yielding to the blessed gush
Of my ungovernable spite,
Have risen up, the red, the old,
Scolding as hard as I could scold.

THE ANNOYER.

"Common as light is love,
And its familiar voice wearies not ever."—SHELLEY.

OVE knoweth everybody's house,
And every human haunt,
And comes unbidden everywhere,
Like people we don't want.
The turnpike-roads and little creeks
Are written with love's words,
And you hear his voice like a thousand bricks
In the lowing of the herds.

He peeps into the teamster's heart,
From his Buena Vista's rim,

And the cracking whips of many men
  Can never frighten him.
He'll come to his cart in the weary night,
  When he's dreaming of his craft;
And he'll float to his eye in the morning light,
  Like a man on a river raft.

He hears the sound of the cooper's adz,
  And makes him, too, his dupe,
For he sighs in his ear from the shaving pile,
  As he hammers on the hoop.
The little girl, the beardless boy,
  The men that walk or stand,
He will get them all in his mighty arms,
  Like the grasp of your very hand.

The shoemaker bangs above his bench,
  And ponders his shining awl,
For love is under the lapstone hid,
  And a spell is on the wall.
It heaves the sole where he drives the pegs,
  And speaks in every blow,
Till the last is dropped from his crafty hand
  And his foot hangs bare below.

He blurs the prints which the shopmen sell,
  And intrudes on the hatter's trade,
And profanes the hostler's stable-yard
  In the shape of the chamber-maid.
In the darkest night and the bright daylight,
  Knowing that he can win,
In every home of good-looking folks
  Will human love come in.

SAMUEL BROWN.

T was many and many a year ago,
In a dwelling down in town,
That a fellow there lived whom you may know,
By the name of Samuel Brown;
And this fellow lived with no other thought
Than to our house come down.

I was a child, and he was a child,
In that dwelling down in town,
But we loved with a love that was more than love,
I and my Samuel Brown,—
With a love that the ladies coveted
Me and Samuel Brown.

And this was the reason that, long ago,
To that dwelling down in town,
A girl came out of her carriage, courting
My beautiful Samuel Brown;
So that her high-bred kinsman came
And bore away Samuel Brown,
And shut him up in a dwelling-house,
In a street quite up in town.

The ladies not half so happy up there,
Went envying me and Brown;
Yes! that was the reason, (as all men know,
In this dwelling down in town),
That the girl came out of the carriage by night,
Coquetting and getting my Samuel Brown.

But our love is more artful by far than the
love
Of those who are older than we,—
Of many far wiser than we,—
And neither the girls that are living above,
Nor the girls that are living in town,
Can ever dissever my soul from the soul
Of the beautiful Samuel Brown.

For the morn never shines without bringing
me lines
From my beautiful Samuel Brown;
And the night's never dark, but I sit in the
park
With my beautiful Samuel Brown.
And often by day, I walk down in Broadway,
With my darling, my darling, my life and
my stay,
To our dwelling down in town,
To our house in the street down town.

GRANNY'S HOUSE.

COMRADES, leave me here a little,
while as yet 'tis early morn,
Leave me here, and when you
want me, sound upon the
dinner-horn.
'Tis the place, and all about it, as of old, the
rat and mouse
Very loudly squeak and nibble, running over
Granny's house;—
Granny's house, with all its cupboards, and
its rooms as neat as wax,

And its chairs of wood unpainted, where the
old cats rubbed their backs,
Many a night from yonder garret window,
ere I went to rest,
Did I see the cows and horses come in slowly
from the west;
Many a night I saw the chickens, flying
upward through the trees,
Roosting on the sleety branches, when I
thought their feet would freeze;
Here about the garden wandered, nourishing
a youth sublime
With the beans, and sweet potatoes, and the
melons which were prime;
When the pumpkin-vines behind me with
their precious fruit reposed,
When I clung about the pear-tree, for the
promise that it closed,
When I dipt into the dinner far as human eye
could see,
Saw the vision of the pie, and all the dessert
that would be.
In the spring a fuller crimson comes upon the
robin's breast;
In the spring the noisy pullet gets herself
another nest;
In the spring a livelier spirit makes the ladies'
tongues more glib;
In the spring a young boy's fancy lightly
hatches up a fib.
Then her cheek was plump and fatter than
should be for one so old,
And she eyed my every motion, with a mute
intent to scold.

And I said, My worthy Granny, now I speak
the truth to thee,—
Better believe it,—I have eaten all the apples
from one tree.
On her kindling cheek and forehead came a
color and a light,
As I have seen the rosy red flashing in the
northern night;
And she turned,—her fist was shaken at the
coolness of the lie;
She was mad, and I could see it, by the
snapping of her eye,
Saying I have hid my feelings, fearing they
should do thee wrong,—
Saying, "I shall whip you, Sammy, whipping,
I shall go it strong!"
She took me up and turned me pretty roughly,
when she'd done,
And every time she shook me, I tried to jerk
and run;
She took off my little coat, and struck again
with all her might,
And before another minute I was free and
out of sight.
Many a morning, just to tease her, did I tell
her stories yet,
Though her whisper made me tingle, when
she told me what I'd get;
Many an evening did I see her where the
willow sprouts grew thick,
And I rushed away from Granny at the touch-
ing of her stick.
O my Granny, old and ugly, O my Granny's
hateful deeds,

O the empty, empty garret, O the garden gone to weeds,
Crosser than all fancy fathoms, crosser than all songs have sung,
I was puppet to your threat, and servile to your shrewish tongue,
Is it well to wish thee happy, having seen thy whip decline
On a boy with lower shoulders, and a narrower back, than mine?
Hark, my merry comrades call me, sounding on the dinner-horn,—
They to whom my Granny's whippings were a target for their scorn;
Shall it not be scorn to me to harp on such a mouldered string?
I am shamed through all my nature to have loved the mean old thing;
Weakness to be wroth with weakness! woman's pleasure, woman's spite,
Nature made them quicker motions, a considerable sight.
Woman is the lesser man, and all thy whippings matched with mine
Are as moonlight unto sunlight, and as water unto wine.
Here at least when I was little, something, O, for some retreat
Deep in yonder crowded city where my life began to beat,
Where one winter fell my father, slipping off a keg of lard,
I was left a trampled orphan, and my case was pretty hard.

Or to burst all links of habit, and to wander
far and fleet,
On from farm-house unto farm-house till I
found my Uncle Pete,
Larger sheds and barns, and newer, and a
better neighborhood,
Greater breadth of field and woodland, and
an orchard just as good.
Never comes my Granny, never cuts her
willow switches there;
Boys are safe at Uncle Peter's, I'll bet you
what you dare.
Hangs the heavy fruited pear-tree: you may
eat just what you like.
'T is a sort of little Eden, about two miles off
the pike.
There, methinks, would be enjoyment, more
than being quite so near
To the place where even in manhood I almost
shake with fear.
There the passions, cramped no longer, shall
have scope and breathing space.
I will 'scape that savage woman, she shall
never rear my race;
Iron-jointed, supple-sinewed, they shall dive
and they shall run;
She has caught me like a wild goat, but she
shall not catch my son.
He shall whistle to the dog, and get the
books from off the shelf,
Not, with blinded eyesight, cutting ugly
whips to whip himself.
Fool again, the dream of fancy! no, I don't
believe it's bliss,

But I'm certain Uncle Peter's is a better place
than this.
Let them herd with narrow foreheads, vacant
of all glorious gains,
Like the horses in the stables, like the sheep
that crop the lanes;
Let them mate with dirty cousins,—what to
me were style or rank,
I the heir of twenty acres, and some money
in the bank?
Not in vain the distance beckons, forward let
us urge our load,
Let our cart-wheels spin till sun-down, ring-
ing down the grooves of road;
Through the white dust of the turnpike she
can't see to give us chase:
Better seven years at uncle's, than fourteen at
Granny's place.
O, I see the blessed promise of my spirit hath
not set!
If we once get in the wagon, we will circum-
vent her yet.
Howsoever these things, be a long farewell to
Granny's farm:
Not for me she'll cut the willows, not at me
she'll shake her arm.
Comes a vapor from the margin, blackening
over heath and holt,
Cramming all the blast before it,—guess it
holds a thunderbolt:
Wish 'twould fall on Granny's house, with
rain, or hail, or fire, or snow,
Let me get my horses started Uncle Peteward,
and I'll go.

"THE DAY IS DONE."

HE day is done, and darkness
From the wing of night is loosed,
As a feather is wafted downward
From a chicken going to roost.

I see the lights of the baker
Gleam through the rain and mist,
And a feeling of sadness comes o'er me,
That I cannot well resist.

A feeling of sadness and *longing*,
That is not like being sick,
And resembles sorrow only
As a brick-bat resembles a brick.

Come, get for me some supper,—
A good and regular meal,
That shall soothe this restless feeling,
And banish the pain I feel.

Not from the pastry baker's,
Not from the shops for cake,
I wouldn't give a farthing
For all that they can make.

For, like the soup at dinner,
Such things would but suggest
Some dishes more substantial,
And to-night I want the best.

Go to some honest butcher,
Whose beef is fresh and nice
As any they have in the city,
And get a liberal slice.

Such things through days of labor,
And nights devoid of ease,
For sad and desperate feelings
Are wonderful remedies.

They have an astonishing power
To aid and reinforce,
And come like the "Finally, brethren,"
That follows a long discourse.

Then get me a tender sirloin
From off the bench or hook,
And lend to its sterling goodness
The science of the cook.

And the night shall be filled with comfort,
And the cares with which it begun
Shall fold up their blankets like Indians,
And silently cut and run.

JOHN THOMPSON'S DAUGHTER.

FELLOW near Kentucky's clime
Cries, "Boatman, do not tarry,
And I'll give thee a silver dime
To row us o'er the ferry."

"Now, who would cross the Ohio,
This dark and stormy water?"
"O, I am this young lady's beau,
And she John Thompson's daughter.

"We've fled before her father's spite
  With great precipitation,
And should he find us here to-night,
  I'd lose my reputation.

"They've missed the girl and purse beside,
  His horsemen hard have pressed me,
And who will cheer my bonny bride,
  If yet they shall arrest me?"

Out spoke the boatman then in time,
  "You shall not fail, don't fear it;
I'll go, not for your silver dime,
  But for your manly spirit.

"And by my word, the bonny bird
  In danger shall not tarry;
For though a storm is coming on,
  I'll row you o'er the ferry."

By this the wind more fiercely rose,
  The boat was at the landing,
And with the drenching rain their clothes
  Grew wet where they were standing.

But still, as wilder rose the wind,
  And as the night grew drearer,
Just back a piece came the police,
  Their tramping sounded nearer.

"O, haste thee, haste!" the lady cries,
  "It's any thing but funny;
I'll leave the light of loving eyes,
  But not my father's money!"

And still they hurried in the face
  Of wind and rain unsparing;
John Thompson reached the landing-place,
  His wrath was turned to swearing.

For by the lightning's angry flash,
  His child he did discover;
One lovely hand held all the cash,
  And one was round her lover!

"Come back, come back," he cried in wo,
  Across the stormy water;
"But leave the purse, and you may go,
  My daughter, O my daughter!"

'Twas vain; they reached the other shore,
  (Such dooms the Fates assign us,)
The gold he piled went with his child,
  And he was left there, *minus.*

GIRLS WERE MADE TO MOURN.

WHEN chill November's surly blast
    Made everybody shiver,
  One evening as I wandered forth,
    Along the Wabash River,
  I spied a woman past her prime,
  Yet with a youthful air,
Her face was covered o'er with curls
  Of *well selected* hair!

Young woman, whither wanderest thou?
  Began the prim old maid;

Are visions of a home to be,
  In all thy dreams displayed?
Or happy wanting but a mate,
  Too soon thou hast began
To wander forth with me to mourn
  The indifference of man!

The sun that overhangs yon fields,
  Outspreading far and wide,
Where thousands by their own hearth sit,
  Or in their carriage ride,—
I've seen yon weary winter sun
  Just forty times return;
And every time has added proofs,
  That girls were made to mourn!

O girls! when in your early years,
  How prodigal of time!
Misspending all your precious hours,
  Your glorious youthful prime!
Thinking to wed just when you please,
  From beau to beau you turn,
Which tenfold force gives nature's law,
  That girls were made to mourn!

Look not on them in youthful prime,
  Ere life's best years are spent!
Man will be gallant to them then,
  And give encouragement!
But see them when they cease to speak
  Of each birthday's return;
Then want and single-blessedness
  Show girls were made to mourn!

A few seem favorites of fate,
  By husband's hands caressed,
But think not all the married folks
  Are likewise truly blest.
For, oh! what crowds, whose lords are out,
  That stay to patch and darn,
Through weary life this lesson learn,
  That girls were made to mourn!

Many and sharp and numerous ills,
  Inwoven with our frame!
More pointed still we make ourselves,
  Regret, remorse, and shame!
And man, whose heaven-erected face
  The smiles of love adorn,—
Man's cold indifference to us
  Makes countless thousands mourn!

If I'm designed to live alone,—
  By nature's law designed,—
Why was this constant wish to wed
  E'er planted in my mind?
If not, why am I subject to
  Man's cruelty or scorn?
Or why has he the will and power
  To make me for him mourn?

See yonder young, accomplished girl,
  Whose words are smooth as oil,
Who'd marry almost any one
  To keep her hands from toil;
But see, the lordly gentleman
  Her favors don't return,
Unmindful though a weeping ma
  And bankrupt father mourn!

Yet, let not this, my hopeful girl,
  Disturb thy youthful breast;
This awful view of woman's fate
  Is surely not the best!
The poor, despised, plain old maid
  Had never sure been born,
Had there not been some recompense
  To comfort those who mourn!

O death! the poor girl's dearest friend,
  The kindest and the best!
Welcome the hour my weary limbs
  Are laid with thee to rest!
The young, the married, fear thy blow
  From hope or husbands torn;
But oh! a blest relief to those
  In single life who mourn!

TO INEZ.

AY, smile not at my garments now;
  Alas! *I* cannot smile again:
Yet Heaven avert that ever thou
  Shouldst dress, and haply dress so plain.

And dost thou ask, Why should I be
  The jest of every foe and friend?
And wilt thou vainly seek to see
  A garb, even thou must fail to mend?

It is not love, it is not hate,
  Nor low Ambition's honors lost,
That bids me loathe my present state,
  And fly from all I loved the most

It is the contrast which will spring
  From all I meet, or hear, or see:
To me no garment tailors bring,—
  Their shops have scarce a charm for me.

It is a something all who rub
  Would know the owner long had wore·
That may not look beyond the tub,
  And can not hope for help before.

What fellow from himself can flee?
  To zones, though more and more remote,
Still, still pursues, where'er I be,
  The blight of life,—the ragged Coat.

Yet others wrapt in broadcloth seem,
  And taste of all that I forsake!
O, may they still of transport dream,
  And ne'er at least like me, awake!

Through many a clime 't is mine to go,
  With many a retrospection curst;
And all my solace is to know,
  Whate'er I wear, I 've worn the worst.

What is the worst? Nay, do not ask,—
  In pity from the search forbear:
Smile on,—nor venture to unclasp
  My Vest, and view the Shirt that's there.

TO MARY.

ELL! thou art happy, and I say
That I should thus be happy too;
For still I hate to go away
As badly as I used to do.

Thy husband's blest,—and 't will impart
Some pangs to view his happier lot;
But let them pass,—O, how my heart
Would hate him, if he clothed thee not.

When late I saw the favorite child,
I thought, like Dutchmen, "I'd go dead,"
But when I saw its breakfast piled,
I thought how much 't would take for bread.

I saw it and repressed my groans
Its father in its face to see,
Because I knew my scanty funds
Were scarce enough for you and me.

Mary, adieu! I must away;
While thou art blest, to grieve were sin,
But near thee I can never stay,
Because I'd get in love again.

I deemed that time, I deemed that pride,
My boyish feeling had subdued,
Nor knew till seated by thy side,
I'd try to get you if I could.

Yet was I calm: I recollect,
My hand had once sought yours again,
But now your husband might object,
And so I kept it on my cane.

I saw thee gaze upon my face,
  Yet meet with neither wo nor scoff;
One only feeling couldst thou trace,
  A disposition to be off.

Away! away, my early dream,
  Remembrance never must awake;
O, where is Mississippi's stream?
  My foolish heart, be still, or break!

THE CHANGE.

N sunset's light o'er Boston thrown,
  A young man proudly stood
Beside a girl, the only one
  He thought was fair or good;
The one on whom his heart was set,
The one he tried so long to get.

He heard his wife's first loving sound,
  A low, mysterious tone,
A music sought, but never found,
  By beaux and gallants gone;
He listened and his heart beat high,—
That was the song of victory!

The rapture of the conqueror's mood
  Rushed burning through his frame,
And all the folks that round him stood
  Its torrents could not tame,
Though stillness lay with eve's last smile
Round Boston Common all the while.

Years came with care; across his life
  There swept a sudden change,
E'en with the one he called his wife,
  A shadow dark and strange,
Breathed from the thought so swift to fall
O'er triumph's hour,—and is this all?

No, more than this! what seemed it *now*
  Right by that one to stand?
A thousand girls of fairer brow
  Walked his own mountain land;
Whence, far o'er matrimony's track,
Their wild, sweet voices called him back.

They called him back to many a glade
  Where once he joyed to rove,
Where often in the beechen shade
  He sat and talked of love;
They called him with their mocking sport
Back to the times he used to court.

But, darkly mingling with the thought
  Of each remembered scene,
Rose up a fearful vision, fraught
  With all that lay between,—
His wrinkled face, his altered lot,
His children's wants, the wife he'd got!

Where was the value of that bride
  He likened once to pearls?
His weary heart within him died
  With yearning for the girls,—
All vainly struggling to repress
That gush of painful tenderness.

He wept; the wife that made his bre.
Beheld the sad reverse,
Even on the spot where he had said
"For better or for worse."
O happiness! how far we flee
Thine own sweet path in search of thee!

"HE NEVER WROTE AGAIN."

HIS hope of publishing went down,
The sweeping press rolled on;
But what was any other crown
To him who hadn't one?
He lived,—for long may mar bewail
When thus he writes in vain:
Why comes not death to those who fail:—
He never wrote again!

Books were put out, and "had a run,"
Like coinage from the mint;
But which could fill the place of one,
That one they wouldn't print?
Before him passed, in calf and sheep,
The thoughts of many a brain;
His lay with the rejected heap:—
He never wrote again!

He sat where men who wrote went round,
And heard the rhymes they built;
He saw their works most richly bound,
With portraits and in gilt.

Dreams of a volume all forgot
  Were blent with every strain:
A thought of one they issued not:—
  He never wrote again!

Minds in that time closed o'er the trace
  Of books once fondly read,
And others came to fill their place,
  And were perused instead.
Tales which young girls had bathed in tears
  Back on the shelves were lain:
Fresh ones came out for other years:—
  He never wrote again!

THE SOIREE.

THIS is the Soiree: from grate to entrance,
  Like milliners' figures, stand the lovely girls;
But from their silent lips no merry sentence
  Disturbs the smoothness of their shining curls.

Ah! what will rise, how will they rally,
  When shall arrive the "gentlemen of ease"!
What brilliant repartee, what witty sally,
  Will mingle with their pleasant symphonies!

I hear even now the infinite sweet chorus,
  The laugh of ecstasy, the merry tone,
That through the evenings that have gone before us
  In long reverberations reach our own.

From round-faced Germans come the guttural voices,
Through curling *moustache* steals the Italian clang,
And, loud amidst their universal noises,
From distant corners sounds the Yankee twang.

I hear the editor, who from his office
Sends out his paper, filled with praise and puff,
And holy priests, who, when they warn the scoffers,
Beat the fine pulpit, lined with velvet stuff.

The tumult of each *saqued*, and charming maiden,
The idle talk that sense and reason drowns,
The ancient dames with jewelry o'erladen,
And trains depending from the brocade gowns,—

The pleasant tone, whose sweetness makes us wonder,
The laugh of gentlemen, and ladies too,
And ever and anon, in tones of thunder,
The diapason of some lady *blue*,—

Is it, O man, with such discordant noises,
With pastimes so ridiculous as these,
Thou drownest Nature's sweet and kindly voices,
And jarrest the celestial harmonies?

Were half the wealth that fills the world with ladies,
  Were half the time bestowed on caps and lace,
Given to the home, the husbands, and the babies,
  There were no time to visit such a place.

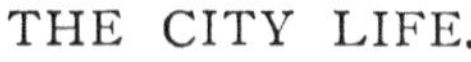

THE CITY LIFE.

OW shall I know thee in that sphere that keeps
  The country youth that to the city goes,
When all of thee, that change can wither, sleeps
  And perishes among your cast-off clothes?

For I shall feel the sting of ceaseless pain,
  If there I met thy one-horse carriage not;
Nor see the hat I love, nor ride again,
  When thou art driving on a gentle trot.

Wilt thou not for me in the city seek,
  And turn to note each passing shawl and gown?
You used to come and see me once a week,—
  Shall I be banished from your thought in town?

In that great street I don't know how to find,
  In the resplendence of that glorious sphere,
And larger movements of the unfettered mind,

Wilt thou forget the love that joined us here?

The love that lived through all the simple past,
And meekly with my country training bore,
And deeper grew, and tenderer to the last,
Shall it expire in town, and be no more?

A happier lot than mine, and greater praise,
Await thee there; for thou, with skill and tact,
Has learnt the wisdom of the world's just ways,
And dressest well, and knowest how to act

For me, the country place in which I dwell
Has made me one of a proscribed band;
And work hath left its scar—that fire of hell
Has left its frightful scar upon my hand.

Yet though thou wear'st the glory of the town,
Wilt thou not keep the same beloved name,
The same black-satin vest, and morning-gown,
Lovelier in New York city, yet the same?

Shalt thou not teach me, in that grander home,
The wisdom that I learned so ill in this,—
The wisdom which is fine,—till I become
Thy fit companion in that place of bliss?

THE MARRIAGE OF SIR JOHN SMITH.

OT a sigh was heard, nor a funeral tone,
As the man to his bridal we hurried;
Not a woman discharged her farewell groan,
On the spot where the fellow was married

We married him just about eight at night,
Our faces paler turning,
By the struggling moonbeam's misty light,
And the gas-lamp's steady burning.

No useless watch-chain covered his vest,
Nor over-dressed we found him;
But he looked like a gentleman wearing his best,
With a few of his friends around him.

Few and short were the things we said,
And we spoke not a word of sorrow,
But we silently gazed on the man that was wed,
And we bitterly thought of the morrow.

We thought, as we silently stood about,
With spite and anger dying,
How the merest stranger had cut us out,
With only half our trying.

Lightly we'll talk of the fellow that's gone,
And oft for the past upbraid him;
But little he'll reck if we let him live on,
In the house where his wife conveyed him.

But our heavy task at length was done,
When the clock struck the hour for retiring;
And we heard the spiteful squib and pun
The girls were sullenly firing.

Slowly and sadly we turned to go,—
We had struggled, and we were human,
We shed not a tear, and we spoke not our wo,
But we left him alone with his woman.

BALLAD OF THE CANAL.

E were crowded in the cabin,
Not a soul had room to sleep;
It was midnight on the waters,
And the banks were very steep.

'Tis a fearful thing when sleeping
To be startled by the shock,
And to hear the rattling trumpet
Thunder, "Coming to a lock!"

So we shuddered there in silence,
For the stoutest berth was shook,
While the wooden gates were opened
And the mate talked with the cook.

As thus we lay in darkness,
Each one wishing we were there,
"We are through!" the captain shouted,
And he sat down on a chair.

And his little daughter whispered,
Thinking that he ought to know,

"Isn't traveling by canal-boats
Just as safe as it is slow?"

Then he kissed the little maiden,
And with better cheer we spoke,
And we trotted into Pittsburg
When the morn looked through the smoke.

I REMEMBER, I REMEMBER.

REMEMBER, I remember,
The house where I was wed,
And the little room from which that night,
My smiling bride was led;
She didn't come a wink too soon,
Nor make too long a stay;
But now I often wish her folks
Had kept the girl away!

I remember, I remember,
Her dresses, red and white,
Her bonnets and her caps and cloaks,—
They cost an awful sight!
The "corner lot" on which I built,
And where my brother met
At first my wife, one washing-day,—
That man is single yet!

I remember, I remember,
Where I was used to court,
And thought that all of married life
Was just such pleasant sport:

My spirit flew in feathers then,
 No care was on my brow;
I scarce could wait to shut the gate,—
 I'm not so anxious now!

I remember, I remember,
 My dear one's smile and sigh;
I used to think her tender heart
 Was close against the sky;
It was a childish ignorance,
 But now it soothes me not
To know I'm farther off from heaven
 Than when she wasn't got!

JACOB.

E dwelt among "aparments let."
 About five stories high;
A man I thought that none would get,
 And very few would try.

A boulder, by a larger stone
 Half hidden in the mud,
Fair as a man when only one
 Is in the neighbourhood.

He lived unknown, and few could tell
 When Jacob was not free;
But he has got a wife,—and O!
 The difference to me!

THE WIFE.

ER washing ended with the day,
Yet lived she at its close,
And passed the long, long night
away,
In darning ragged hose.

But when the sun in all his state
Illumed the eastern skies,
She passed about the kitchen grate,
And went to making pies.

A PSALM OF LIFE.

WHAT THE HEART OF THE YOUNG
WOMAN SAID TO THE OLD MAID.

ELL me not, in idle jingle,
Marriage is an empty dream,
For the girl is dead that's single,
And things are not what they
seem.

Married life is real, earnest;
Single blessedness a fib;
Taken from man, to man returnest,
Has been spoken of the rib.

Not enjoyment, and not sorrow,
Is our destined end or way;
But to act, that each to-morrow
Nearer brings the wedding-day.

Life is long, and youth is fleeting,
And our hearts, if there we search,
Still like steady drums are beating
Anxious marches to the church.

In the world's broad field of battle,
In the bivouac of life,
Be not like dumb, driven cattle!
Be a woman, be a wife!

Trust no Future, howe'er pleasant!
Let the dead Past bury its dead!
Act,—act in the living Present:
Heart within, and MAN ahead!

Lives of married folks remind us
We can live our lives as well,
And, departing, leave behind us
Such examples as will tell;—

Such examples, that another,
Sailing far from Hymen's port,
A forlorn, unmarried brother,
Seeing, shall take heart, and court.

Let us then be up and doing,
With the heart and head begin;
Still achieving, still pursuing,
Learn to labor, and to win!

"THERE'S A BOWER OF BEAN-VINES."

THERE'S a bower of bean-vines in Benjamin's yard,
And the cabbages grow round it, planted for greens;
In the time of my childhood 'twas terribly hard
To bend down the bean-poles, and pick off the beans.

That bower and its products I never forget,
But oft, when my landlady presses me hard,
I think, are the cabbages growing there yet,
Are the bean-vines still bearing in Benjamin's yard?

No, the bean-vines soon withered that once used to wave,
But some beans had been gathered, the last that hug on,
And a soup was distilled in a kettle, that gave
All the fragrance of summer when summer was gone.

Thus memory draws from delight, ere it dies,
An essence that breathes of it awfully hard:
And thus good to my taste as 't was then to my eyes,
Is that bower of bean-vines in Benjamin's yard.

"WHEN LOVELY WOMAN."

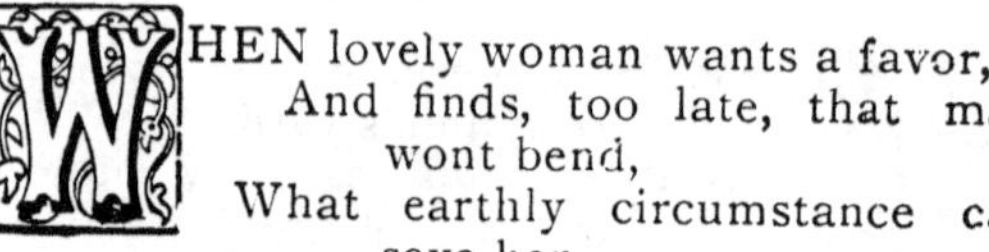

WHEN lovely woman wants a favor,
And finds, too late, that man wont bend,
What earthly circumstance can save her
From disappointment in the end?

The only way to bring him over
The last experiment to try,
Whether a husband or a lover,
If he have feeling, is, to cry!

SHAKESPERIAN READINGS.

H, but to fade, and live we know not where,
To be a cold obstruction and to groan!
This sensible, warm woman to become
A prudish clod; and the delighted spirit
To live and die alone, or to reside
With married sisters, and to have the care
Of half a dozen children, not your own;
And driven, for no one wants you,
Round about the pendant world; or worse than worse
Of those that disappointment and pure spite
Have driven to madness: 'T is too horrible!
The weariest and most troubled married life

That age, ache, penury, or jealousy
Can lay on nature, is a paradise
To being an old maid.

That very time I saw, (but thou couldst not,)
Walking between the garden and the barn,
Reuben, all armed; a certain aim he took
At a young chicken, standing by a post,
And loosed his bullet smartly from his gun,
As he would kill a hundred thousand hens.
But I might see young Reuben's fiery shot
Lodged in the chaste board of the garden
fence,
And the domesticated fowl passed on,
In henly meditation, bullet free.

My father had a daughter got a man,
As it might be, perhaps, were I good-looking,
I should, your lordship.
And what's her residence?
A hut, my lord, she never owned a house,
But let her husband, like a graceless scamp,
Spend all her little means,—she thought she
ought,—
And in a wretched chamber, on an alley,
She worked like masons on a monument,
Earning their bread. Was not this love
indeed?

www.ingramcontent.com/pod-product-compliance
Lightning Source LLC
LaVergne TN
LVHW011216110826
845150LV00006B/1442

* 9 7 8 1 4 2 5 5 1 6 9 4 9 *